Advances in Contemporary Educational Thought Series

Jonas F. Soltis, Editor

UNDERSTANDING EQUAL EDUCATIONAL OPPORTUNITY

Social Justice, Democracy, and Schooling

KENNETH R. HOWE

Teachers College, Columbia University
New York and London

To my mother, Elizabeth

Published by Teachers College Press, 1234 Amsterdam Avenue, New York, NY 10027

Library of Congress Cataloging-in-Publication Data

Howe, Kenneth Ross.
    Understanding equal educational opportunity : social justice, democracy, and schooling / Kenneth R. Howe.
        p.   cm. — (Advances in contemporary educational thought series ; v. 20)
    Includes bibliographical references and index.
    ISBN 0-8077-3600-7 (cloth : alk. paper). — ISBN 0-8077-3599-X (pbk. : alk. paper)
    1. Educational equalization—United States.   2. Multicultural education—United States.   3. Segregation in education—United States.   4. Sex discrimination in education—United States.
5. School choice—United States.   I. Title.   II. Series.
LC213.2.H69   1997
379.2′6′0973—dc21   96-37710

ISBN 0-8077-3599-X (paper)
ISBN 0-8077-3600-7 (cloth)

Printed on acid-free paper
Manufactured in the United States of America

04   03   02   01   00   99   98   97   8   7   6   5   4   3   2   1

Contents

Foreword

We have become much more politically sophisticated in the 20th century, realizing that providing a system of compulsory, free public education for all does not necessarily provide equal educational opportunity for all. The physical and financial aspects of public schools differ markedly. In school plant and dollars per pupil, there *are* "savage inequalities." Many children of the poor, of minorities, of different cultures come to school unprepared to learn; de facto school segregation still exists; and tracking, putting people "in their place," still is a dominant educational practice.

In this book, Kenneth Howe digs deeply into the complex idea of equality of educational opportunity. He reveals many subtleties and problems that need to be understood if this basic democratic principle is to serve us in our quest to provide an education that keeps the future open for our children. Key issues of today—multiculturalism, gender, segregation, tracking, special and gifted education, testing, school choice—are carefully and thoughtfully examined with regard to their impact on attempts to provide equal educational opportunity. A host of recent policies and practices aimed at reforming education are measured against the standard of equity by Howe, and found wanting.

This is a critical book, but also a hopeful one. Providing genuine equality of educational opportunity is not easy, or completely attainable. In fact, to think of it as a goal, as something we should try to accomplish by restructuring public schools, may be the wrong way to think about how to approach this important democratic ideal in practice. This ideal might better serve as the basis for a subsidiary question that needs to be asked of every proposed educational reform. Regardless of what a reform is designed to accomplish, we should ask, How will it affect the equality of educational opportunity of students in any school adopting the reform? In this way, the ideal can serve a much needed watchdog function when we are preoccupied with other desirable goals.

In order to be able to answer this question, we need to have a clear understanding of what we mean by equality of educational opportunity, and this is the positive contribution of Howe's book. It provides a rich interpretation of what equal educational opportunity *should* mean. It develops this interpretation by philosophically arguing against other, competing interpretations in use today that are embedded in contemporary policies and practices. Howe offers what he calls a radical liberal theory of democracy, social justice, and schooling to serve as the basis for detecting the presence or absence of equal educational opportunity. His is a well thought out and sophisticated theory that many will see as ultimately fair and just. Others may disagree with his ideas and arguments, but there is no doubt that Howe has provided in this work a genuine basis for advance in our contemporary educational thought and debate about equality of educational opportunity in our schools.

Jonas F. Soltis
Series Editor

Preface

My interest in equality of educational opportunity was prompted in the late 1980s, when, after having spent several years in a medical school, I took a faculty position in the School of Education at Boulder. In the process of learning my way around the education arena, I was struck by the prominence accorded to the principle of equality of educational opportunity. It was a pervasive topic of conversation not only in the literature—on gender, tracking, and bilingual education, for example, the issues I encountered first—but also among practicing public school teachers and administrators.

I was also struck by how widely interpretations of the principle varied. The literature employed it in shifting ways, even within the same book or article. Sometimes it was clearly identified with equality of access, sometimes with compensatory measures, and sometimes (less clearly) with equality of results. Many schoolteachers and administrators identified it with sameness, as in "I treat all my students the same." Others were more inclined to identify it with treating students differently, in response to their different needs. Still others, who seemed to have no reservations about using it, were genuinely puzzled when asked to explain just what equality of educational opportunity meant.

These two observations about how the concept operated—its prominence coupled with its pervasive ambiguity—provided the impetus for this book and helped determine the shape it has taken. My challenge from the beginning was to strike a balance between faithfulness to philosophy and faithfulness to the vocabulary and empirical research that drive contemporary policy debates in education. Seeing the challenge in this way fits with my general view of philosophy of education: It should be thoroughly grounded in philosophical reflection but nonetheless speak to a broad audience of educators in order to inform the contemporary debates surrounding educational policy and practice.

Thus I have quite self-consciously chosen a number of influential authors—James Coleman, Jonathan Kozol, E. D. Hirsch, Arthur Schlesinger, Jeannie Oakes, and John Chubb and Terry Moe, for instance—and government reform proposals—*A Nation at Risk, America 2000, the*

NCEST Report, and *Goals 2000*—that a general education audience is likely to be familiar with but that are not philosophical in any customary sense. And I have not treated the views expressed as if they were at the periphery of my more strictly philosophical concerns but have given them a central place, often using them to frame the issues I address.

Still, this book is strongly—primarily—philosophical in its approach. Very early on I identify an important part of the problem of achieving equality of educational opportunity with first deciding how to *interpret the concept.* How else can we know what goal to shoot for or when we attain it? And isn't *some* interpretation always there, even if only implicitly? The emphasis on getting the conceptual terrain mapped out is just the sort of activity (though not the only one) with which philosophy has been historically associated. Thus, although I credit James Coleman (a sociologist) with having done a good deal to bring the issue of interpretation to the fore—as well as with the provocative idea that equality of educational opportunity might be identified with equality of educational results—I turn to philosophy for illumination.

With the possible exception of John Dewey, the philosophers I turn to are likely to be less familiar to a general audience than the authors mentioned above. In addition to Dewey, those who figure most prominently are John Rawls, Amy Gutmann, and Will Kymlicka (all liberals), Nel Noddings (a care theorist), and Iris Marion Young (a critical theorist/radical democrat).

This book sets forth a radical liberal theory of democracy, justice, and schooling. Why ''radical''? What can it mean when attached to ''liberal''? After trying out some other descriptions (I settled on ''contemporary liberal theory'' for a while), I decided that ''radical'' (borrowed from Dewey) best calls to attention a widespread misconstrual of what liberal theory has to offer. And it is this: Liberal *theory* is often implicitly identified with liberalism as it is *in fact* exemplified in current arrangements; then both are written off as hopelessly compensatory, paternalistic, oppressive, and otherwise thoroughly bankrupt.

But this papers over a clear and important distinction. No less than other ''radicals,'' liberal theorists can be (and are) deeply critical of liberalism *in fact,* including the institution of public schooling and the cultural, political, and economic structures that so heavily influence it. Liberal theorists need not be (and are not) mere apologists for the status quo or advocates of only the most minimal kind of Band-Aid remedies. Instead, they are in an advantageous position to foster radical change because of the foothold they have in the vocabulary and traditions of the political community.

But now I have embarked on the argument.

Acknowledgments

It is difficult for me to say when I actually began this book, and therefore whom I should thank. On the other hand, just when I began my analysis of the concept of equality of educational opportunity is quite easy to pin down. So let me begin there.

In the summer of 1988, with the encouragement and support of Jim Nickel, I received a Junior Faculty Development Award from the University of Colorado at Boulder. This resulted in my first article on the topic, "In Defense of Outcomes-Based Conceptions of Equality of Educational Opportunity," published in 1989 in *Educational Theory*. Soon after, in 1990, Nick Burbules published a biting rejoinder, also in *Educational Theory*. Although I am still not prepared to concede to Nick that my analysis committed me to what he claimed it did, I will concede (effectively have conceded) that the analysis encouraged puzzlement and (in my view) misinterpretation. I thank Nick for stimulating me to reformulate my analysis in a way that rendered it more effective.

By this time, the idea for this book was beginning to take shape. In 1990 I won a Spencer Foundation postdoctoral fellowship, and the support it provided was essential in getting my project off the ground.

Ken Strike was the first to see the formal prospectus. I thank him for his (always) incisive comments and his suggestion that I approach Jonas Soltis with the idea of publishing the book in the Advances in Contemporary Educational Thought series. I thank Jonas for his receptiveness and encouragement, and for his substantive comments on my (by this time) revised prospectus (Ken also provided a second round of comments).

I also wish to thank several colleagues and students at the University of Colorado at Boulder who read various portions of the book, engaged me in useful conversation, or both. These include Margaret Eisenhart, Ernie House, Dan Liston, Scott Marion, Lorrie Shepard, and Michelle Moses (who read and provided helpful comments on all of the chapters), as well as students in the fall 1995 general doctoral seminar (especially Anastasia Brelias), my fall 1996 philosophy of education course, and my spring 1994 seminar in equality of educational opportunity. I also thank Linda Webster for helping me put the reference list together and cleaning up the rest.

I adapted several articles and book chapters that I published along the way. Because none of these straightforwardly corresponds to any chapter of the book, I acknowledge the journals and collections in question by indicating the sections of chapters for which they have been adapted. Where the adaptation is reasonably extensive and faithful, I use "is adapted from"; otherwise, I use "borrows from."

Chapter 2. The section The Criterion of Equal Results: Political, Not Metaphysical borrows from "Equality of Educational Opportunity as Equality of Educational Outcomes," *Philosophy of Education 1989* (Normal, IL: Philosophy of Education Society, 1990), pp. 292–299; the section Equality of Educational Results, Equality of Educational Opportunity, and Liberal Theories of Justice is adapted from a portion of "In Defense of Outcomes-based Conceptions of Equal Educational Opportunity," *Educational Theory*, 39(4), 317–336 (1989); the section The Participatory Interpretation of Equality of Educational Opportunity and the Criterion of Equal Educational Worth is adapted from "Equality of Educational Opportunity and the Criterion of Equal Educational Worth," *Studies in Philosophy and Education*, 11, 329–337 (1993).

Chapter 4. The section The Abandonment of Universal Educational Ideals borrows from "Currents in the Conversation About Diversity," *Educational Theory*, 45(4), 525–539 (1995).

Chapter 5. The section Special Education is adapted from a portion of "Educational Ethics, Social Justice, and Children With Disabilities," in C. Christensen and F. Rizvi (Eds.), *Disability and the Dilemmas of Education and Justice* (Philadelphia: Open University Press, 1996).

Chapter 6. The section Validity, Bias, and Justice in Educational Testing: The Limits of a Consequentialist Conception is adapted from an article of the same name, in A. Neiman (Ed.), *Philosophy of Education 1995* (Normal, IL: Philosophy of Education Society, 1996), pp. 295–302. The remainder of Chapter 6 is adapted from "Standards, Assessment, and Equality of Educational Opportunity," *Educational Researcher*, 23(8), 27–33 (1994).

Chapter 8. A portion of Chapter 8 borrows from "Democracy, Justice, and Action Research: Some Theoretical Developments," *Educational Action Research*, 3(3), 347–349 (1995).

I end these acknowledgments with special thanks to Tonda Potts, my wife. She tolerated well my aloofness and detachment when I was immersed, as well as my occasional defensiveness toward her urgings to make my arguments accessible. But most of all, her genuine interest in me and what I do helped in no small way to make the completion of this book something worth wanting.

CHAPTER 1

Overview

*Liberalism must now become radical, meaning by "radical" percep-
tion of the necessity of thorough-going changes in the set-up of institutions and corresponding activity to bring changes to pass.*
　　　　　　　　　　　—*John Dewey, "Renascent Liberalism"*

The ideal of equality of opportunity has long been central to the project
of liberalism. As the 20th century has unfolded, the link between equality of opportunity per se and equality of educational opportunity in
particular has grown steadily in importance, so much so that promoting
equality of educational opportunity has been the foremost mission of
U.S. educational policy through much of the second half of this century.
Spurred by the celebrated *Brown v. Board of Education* decision in 1954,
the quest for equality of educational opportunity has been extended
from its original focus on race to encompass other sources of discrimina-
tion such as disability, language, and gender. The upshot has been a
plethora of lawsuits, congressional legislation, and social and educational programs on behalf of groups who have been—and are being—
denied equality of opportunity within the U.S. educational system.

By any reasonable measure, the drive for equality of educational
opportunity must be judged an abject failure. As Jonathan Kozol (1991)
reveals in *Savage Inequalities*, even in terms of the minimally demanding
measure of school finance, the current state of U.S. public education
vis-à-vis equality is shocking: Expenditures currently range from roughly $2,000 to roughly $20,000 per pupil. Contrary to the much overused
slogan that "you can't solve problems by throwing money at them,"
the effects of inadequate funding are quite easy to discern. Consider
what it means to be a student in a school in East St. Louis—where
sewage has a habit of backing up into kitchens and bathrooms; where
there are "scores of windows without glass"; where "you can smell the
urinals a hundred feet away"; and where there is a constant threat that
further cuts in funding will make things even worse (pp. 36–37).

An important source of such inequality, no doubt, is the general lack of the *political will* to embrace and see egalitarian values through, a problem fueled by the burgeoning influence of the political right over the last several decades (Apple, 1993a). This is the essence of the analysis offered by Kozol (1991), who asserts that public schooling policy "has been turned back one hundred years" (p. 4) as a consequence of the Reagan era. This analysis is correct as far as it goes, but it neglects an underlying problem that has, since long before Reagan took office, obstructed the drive for educational equality: the lack of *political understanding* of what equality of educational opportunity requires.

James Coleman (1968) identified this problem early in the post-*Brown* era in the course of interpreting the results of his landmark study of educational equality. In particular, he observed that the concept of equality of educational opportunity has a variety of interpretations and that empirical data mean different things and have different implications for educational policy, depending on which interpretation is employed. For example, equal inputs is a different and less demanding criterion than equal results;[1] equal results is a different and less demanding criterion when it adjusts for factors such as income than when it does not; and equal results is a different and less demanding criterion when it seeks equality among groups than when it seeks equality among individuals. In general, Coleman points out that (a) how efforts to promote equality of educational opportunity are to be assessed and (b) what steps might be taken to remedy identified shortcomings are difficult questions to answer—not just because of their empirical complexity but because of their philosophical complexity as well.

However obvious Coleman's observation, it has gone largely unheeded in discussions of equality of educational opportunity. Coleman's challenge to take seriously the problem of how to interpret equality of educational opportunity, particularly his suggestion that it might be (or should be) interpreted in terms of equal results, was all too easily dismissed (Howe, 1989). Interest in his question waned soon after he raised it, and the concept of equality of educational opportunity reverted to, as J. R. Lucas says, a "witch's brew of vagueness and equivocation" (in Levin, 1981).

Today, educational scholars from across the political spectrum employ the concept of equality of educational opportunity as if its intended meaning were transparent—and it almost never is. As a current example, consider the controversy raging about "cultural literacy." E. D. Hirsch (1988), one of the most visible participants in the controversy, believes that equality of educational opportunity can be achieved for historically disadvantaged groups only by instilling in them the received view of cultural literacy. By contrast, Hirsch's detractors (I among them)

believe that equal educational opportunity can be achieved for historically disadvantaged groups only by suspending judgment on cultural
literacy and by providing them with an equal voice in negotiating what
it should be. On this view, Hirsch's proposal is worse than ineffectual.
It constitutes an obstacle to equality of educational opportunity for those
groups historically excluded from participation.

A general and inarticulate commitment to equality of educational
opportunity, then, doesn't take us very far in the direction of understanding what it requires, or, accordingly, very far in the direction of
specific policies and practices. For such a general commitment may
merely disguise tacit but significant differences in underlying philosophical assumptions.[2] Where such assumptions are not articulated,
policies that putatively promote equality of educational opportunity are
at best blind and at worst pointing down a path that leads in altogether
the wrong direction.

ORGANIZATION OF BOOK

This book has two general aims: to develop a general conception of
equality of educational opportunity, and to employ it to characterize the
various problems now confronting public education in the United States
and to evaluate the policies proposed to solve them. Chapter 2, "A
Radical Liberal Framework," is devoted almost exclusively to the first
aim; Chapters 3 and 4, "Gender" and "Multiculturalism," are devoted
to both aims; and Chapters 5, 6, and 7, "Segregation," "Testing," and
"School Choice," are devoted almost exclusively to the second aim.

I begin Chapter 2 by considering what I call the "received view" on
the interpretation of equality of educational opportunity: that equality
of educational opportunity is one kind of principle and equality of educational results quite another. Against this view, I set out to establish
that educational opportunities and educational results cannot be disentangled. For having *real* educational opportunities—*educational opportunities worth wanting*—requires that certain results have been previously
attained. A child who has not yet learned to read, for instance, has
no *real* opportunity to proceed through the subsequent levels of the
curriculum that depend on reading. Such a child has merely a *bare*[3]
opportunity to further his or her education, an opportunity in name
only. Given this observation, the problem of the relationship between
equality of educational opportunity and equality of educational results
should not be framed, as in the received view, in terms of *whether*
educational results should be equalized in the name of equality of edu-

cational opportunity. It should be framed instead in terms of *what kind* of educational results should be equalized and *to what degree*.

The remainder of Chapter 2 is devoted to providing a general response to these two questions and to developing a general conceptual framework for the remaining chapters. First, I defend liberal-egalitarianism against its libertarian and utilitarian rivals.[4] What most distinguishes liberal-egalitarianism from these other two perspectives is that it places a principled limit on the degree to which the goal of equal educational opportunity can be traded for other goals of public education with which it sometimes competes, such as maximizing economic productivity (in the case of utilitarianism) and minimizing state intervention (in the case of libertarianism). Heavily influenced by Amy Gutmann (1987), I identify this principled limit with a threshold level of educational attainment, to be distinguished from strict equality. This limit is further distinguished from strict equality by its emphasis on the skills and knowledge most closely associated with effective democratic citizenship.

Next, I describe and evaluate three interpretations of equality of educational opportunity: formal, compensatory, and participatory. The formal interpretation eschews equalizing educational results and is most closely associated with libertarianism. I reject it for both reasons. The compensatory interpretation seeks to equalize educational results by compensating for the disadvantages experienced by various groups and can take either a utilitarian or a liberal-egalitarian form. The liberal-egalitarian form is superior in my view, but along with the utilitarian form it is vulnerable to a common objection: The compensatory interpretation is insensitive to the needs, interests, and perspectives of historically excluded groups in determining what ''disadvantages'' should be compensated for—that is, in determining what educational opportunities are worth wanting. Thus the compensatory interpretation is implicitly grounded in the goal of assimilation and comes at the expense of genuine democracy.

The participatory interpretation seeks to overcome the defect in the compensatory interpretation by building into the principle of equality of educational opportunity the requirement to include the needs, interests, and perspectives of all groups—especially groups that have been historically excluded—in determining what educational opportunities are indeed worth wanting. How the participatory interpretation unites equality of educational opportunity with democracy and justice and how it provides liberal educational theory with a response to piercing contemporary challenges are central themes of this book.

The specific issues I consider in the subsequent chapters—gender, multiculturalism, segregation, testing, choice—are highly interrelated. My reason for treating them separately is dictated more by historical contingency than by abstract logic. It just so happens that distinct conversations have evolved around these issues, at different times, with different emphases, and at different levels of scholarly effort. Furthermore, and no doubt related to these observations, educational policy is fragmented in the same way.

In Chapter 3, I document the inequality of educational results between boys and girls and men and women and the broader consequences this has. I then quickly entertain and reject two apologies for such inequality: that it may be attributed to natural differences between the sexes and that it is the result of free choice. The appeal to natural differences is an all too facile attempt to derive the way things ought to be from the way things always have been, reminiscent of the kind of apology once given for the institution of slavery. It ignores the very complex relationship between social arrangements and the skills, attitudes, talents, and identities that group members form. The appeal to choice is subject to a closely related criticism: It ignores the social circumstances that have historically shaped the "contexts of choice"[5] available to girls and women.

I next look to feminism for guidance in developing an interpretation of equality of educational opportunity that may genuinely include girls and women. I compare "humanist" (or "liberal") feminism with "gynocentric" (or "relational") feminism.[6] Humanist feminism is at best compensatory and thus suffers from difficulties already alluded to. Gynocentric feminism escapes this problem only at the expense of incurring problems of its own. By celebrating the skills, dispositions, and activities historically associated with women, this brand of feminism makes it difficult to understand how women are oppressed, and by supplanting the (male) concern with justice with the (female) concern for caring, justice seems to go by the boards altogether. The way out of this impasse is to incorporate the insights of both humanist and gynocentric feminism into a participatory conception of equality of educational opportunity that, if adhered to, would transform educational arrangements in the direction of gender equality. I illustrate how this can be accomplished by reconciling the (liberal) theory of Amy Gutmann (1987) with the (relational) theory of Nel Noddings (1992).

In Chapter 4, I frame the problem of multicultural education in terms of how to respond to the fact that, as education is presently structured, doing well in school exacts greater "opportunity costs"—in terms of one's identity and continued participation in one's cultural group—from members of certain groups than from members of others.

The phenomenon of African Americans' "acting White" is an important case in point. (See, e.g., Fordham, 1993.) I then entertain three ways of responding to this problem: by adopting traditional universal educational ideals and educating all children in terms of them (the melting pot view); by abandoning universal educational ideals as inherently hegemonic and oppressive (the postmodernist view); or by developing some educational ideals that though universal, are sufficiently open to cultural differences to avoid oppression (the participatory view).

I use E. D. Hirsch's (1988) view to exemplify the melting pot view and challenge his claims that inculcating "cultural literacy," based on the status quo, is in the best interests of both the nation and those who must do the melting. In particular, his argument that extra costs must be exacted from members of certain groups because the only alternative is tribalism and the Tower of Babel is quite dubious, particularly where the goal of participatory democracy is taken to supersede goals such as economic efficiency.

I criticize postmodernism for going too far in the other direction. That is, insofar as it rejects universal educational ideals in toto, a consequence of rejecting the rational principles that underlie them, it is condemned to moral-political silence regarding what a just and democratic educational system would look like. (In addition to the argument in Chapter 4, I return briefly to this point later in this chapter.)

I develop the participatory view in opposition to both the melting pot and postmodernist views, but I take a lesson from each. Against melting pot thinkers, I agree with postmodernist thinkers that the question of educational ideals has to be opened up for negotiation. Ignoring the voices of historically excluded groups and foisting the traditional curriculum on these groups is indeed oppressive. Against postmodernists, however, I agree with melting pot thinkers that *some* universal educational ideals must be settled on if the quest for a just and democratic educational system is to be coherent.

I take Amy Gutmann's (1987)"democratic threshold" as a first approximation to the kind of universal educational ideal that is required. (In this way, the analysis of Chapter 4 extends those of Chapters 2 and 3, where I also make liberal use of Gutmann's views.) I embrace her general approach of grounding equality of educational opportunity in the requirements of political equality but find her specific proposal wanting in several ways. First, "democratic character"—the general place-holder for the knowledge, skills, and dispositions associated with her threshold—relies on the too weak virtue of tolerance. It needs to be augmented with the "virtue of recognition,"[7] which goes beyond merely "putting up with" cultural differences to include something more akin to respect. Second, the "principle of nonrepression"—a procedural constraint on negotiating educational ideals as well as a pedagogical principle—is likewise too weak. It needs to be supplanted with a principle of nonoppression, which goes beyond merely letting people speak their minds to insuring that legitimate claims have real authority. I end Chapter 4 by illustrating and testing the "participatory ideal" I develop in terms of the guidance it provides in judging the merit of claims advanced by various groups that public schools are oppressive— for instance, gay and lesbian youth versus Christian fundamentalists.

I begin Chapter 5 with a very brief discussion of between-school segregation and then move quickly to its within-school forms. I identify three: tracking, gifted education, and special education.

Tracking is typically defended as serving the interests of all students (the "best interests" rationale), serving the interests (particularly economic) of the nation overall (the "utilitarian" rationale), or both. The best interests rationale may be dismissed as inconsistent with the empirical evidence. The research findings point unequivocally to the conclusion that tracking unavoidably trades the quality of educational opportunities associated with some tracks for the quality of those associated with others. (Under existing arrangements, high-track students almost always benefit.)

The utilitarian rationale embraces the idea that trade-offs must be made, and it invokes its principle of maximizing total benefit to determine just what these trade-offs should be: higher-quality opportunities for the more talented in exchange for lower-quality opportunities for the less talented. This is the most efficient way to develop needed "human capital." Because it provides no assurance that all students receive an adequate education, up to some threshold, the utilitarian rationale for tracking is unjust as well as antidemocratic.

Gifted education appeals to the same two rationales as tracking, and, accordingly, suffers from the same difficulties. There are several twists, however. The utilitarian rationale for gifted education faces the difficulty of devising a defensible construct and an accurate means of identification, something gifted-education proponents have not managed to do. The best interests rationale faces the difficulty of making good on the alleged analogy between gifted and special education based on the claim that they both serve special needs. That this analogy is tenuous is shown by the fact that the way gifted programs respond to the "special needs" of the gifted is to give them a better version of the curriculum, more of it, and at an accelerated rate. Furthermore, the worry in special education is the *over*representation of minorities and boys. That the worry in gifted education is the *under*representation of minorities and girls is telling.

The section on special education is couched explicitly in terms of the formal, compensatory, and participatory interpretations of equality of educational opportunity. Formal and compensatory interpretations prove inadequate here for the kinds of reasons discussed several times already. On the other hand, special education provides the vehicle to clarify an important point about the compensatory interpretation, namely, that what makes it objectionable is its "normalizing" (in Foucault's sense) thrust. Where those receiving compensation endorse what is being done in its name, say, by gladly accepting a hearing aid, compensation is not nearly so problematic. Indeed, it dovetails with the participatory interpretation.

Special education also provides the vehicle for clarifying the demands of the participatory ideal. In particular, the participatory ideal is out of reach for children with certain kinds of disabilities. To take one of the examples I discuss, consider a child with "significantly limited intellectual capacity," who is highly unlikely to be able to master the knowledge and reasoning skills associated with democratic deliberation. In cases like this, I endorse the suggestion that such children be included in the regular classroom, in order that they may learn general social skills, to care and be cared for, and to enjoy the benefits of belonging. Inclusive practices serve to foster the virtue of recognition in all children, and I see no inconsistency in adopting more modest aims for certain children vis-à-vis the participatory ideal while maintaining a general commitment to it.

Pressures to segregate children through tracking, gifted education, and special education are here to stay so long as educational achievement continues to be the ticket to expanded opportunity, public education continues to be seen as mired in mediocrity, and inadequate funding continues to force difficult choices. Unfortunately, two of the most prominent reform proposals—rigorous standards/testing regimens and school choice—do nothing to alleviate these pressures. On the contrary, they exacerbate them.

In Chapter 6, I evaluate what various proposals to implement more rigorous standards and testing imply for equality of educational opportunity. The argument has two strands.

In the first, I consider the issue of how testing for the purposes of distributing educational opportunities is unavoidably implicated in justice. Historically, rendering testing consistent with equality of educational opportunity has been associated with eliminating bias, where bias is identified with a poor correlation between test scores and the performance they purport to predict. Bias in this sense, "predictive bias," is associated with denying equality of educational opportunity, to be sure, but eliminating it is not sufficient to eliminate the problem. For the performance itself, the "criterion," may itself be biased, in terms of race or gender, for example. What this implies is that testing cannot be rendered consistent with equality of educational opportunity in the absence of eliminating "criterion bias"—in the absence, that is, of eliminating bias from the curriculum. And this is a problem that the recent moves toward "consequentialist" conceptions of validity and "performance assessment" do little or nothing to solve.

In the second strand of argument of Chapter 6, I examine the more obvious connections between testing and equality of educational opportunity, in terms of recent celebrated reform proposals. The proposals of the Reagan-Bush era, to be found in *A Nation at Risk* (The National Commission on Excellence in Education, 1983) and *America 2000* (U.S. Department of Education, 1991), incorporate a formal interpretation of equality of educational opportunity and largely ignore the problem of the injustice involved in holding students responsible for the curriculum when they may have had little opportunity to master it. Subsequent proposals, such as the National Council of Education Standards and Testing [NCEST] report (1992) and the Clinton administration's *Goals 2000* (U.S. House of Representatives, 1994b), seek to remedy this defect by not holding students responsible in the absence of insuring that "opportunity to learn standards" have been met. These proposals are problematic because they incorporate a compensatory interpretation of equality of educational opportunity and tie compensation to the traditional curriculum.

A necessary condition of squaring testing with equality of educational opportunity is a wholesale renegotiation of educational aims, pedagogical practices, and curricular content. Democratic citizenship needs to be taken seriously rather than merely given lip service, and educational opportunities must move beyond being merely formal (and empty) or compensatory (and costly). The alternative, narrow focus on standards and testing is more a diversion from the problems that beset public education than a solution to them.

In Chapter 7, I examine school choice. I identify four different rationales: strong parental autonomy, the market, communitarian, and pragmatic.

The strong parental autonomy rationale takes two forms: libertarian and moral conservative. In the extreme, the libertarian form is opposed to virtually any state interference in how parents see fit to raise and educate their children. Thus parents should have complete freedom in determining what schools (if any) their children attend and what (if anything) they are taught. But this practice is untenable. Not just in education but in other areas—health care and labor, for instance—parents are not permitted to do anything they please with or to their children. When libertarians moderate their view, as they must, the question shifts from *whether* the state should have any say in children's education to *how far* the state's influence should go. This takes the ball out of the libertarian's court.

In contrast to the libertarian form, which is principled, the moral conservative form is strategic. At bottom, moral conservatives do not believe in strong parental autonomy. They would if they could (and many try to) reform public education to inculcate their vision of the good and moral life in all children, and they would do so with no compunctions about overriding the autonomy of parents with whom they disagreed. For moral conservatives, then, school choice is simply a device for insuring that at least their own children get the kind of education of which they approve. This, their true reason for supporting school choice, lies hidden behind the rhetoric of parental autonomy.

The market rationale for school choice is a good deal more difficult to pin down and evaluate from among the four rationales I consider. I use Chubb and Moe's (1990) *Politics, Markets and America's Schools* as my primary foil. Among the criticisms I advance are the following: They employ an impoverished conception of democracy; incoherently combine free market libertarianism and utilitarianism; consistently rely on highly suspect and distorted empirical claims; wrongly identify free markets with democracy; ignore the problems inherent in construing education as a private rather than a public good; and give far too little attention to the implications of their proposal for equality of educational opportunity.

The arguments are too many and too detailed to rehearse at the same level I have so far employed in this overview. In the end, I merely confirm my strong initial suspicion. If education is distributed in the same way automobiles are distributed, the resulting pattern will be the same: Some consumers will get Cadillac educations, some will get Yugo educations, and some will wind up on foot. In addition to the moral problem inherent in such inequality, it renders democracy a sham.

The communitarian rationale sees expanded school choice as the key to responding to the diversity that currently characterizes U.S. public education. It sees as ineffective and morally objectionable cookie-cutter schools that attempt to inculcate in all children the knowledge and skills deemed appropriate by the powers that be—schools, moreover, are generally inflexible in how they go about this. But, in contrast to the unfettered liberty promoted by the libertarian rationale and the consumer preferences promoted by the market rationale (their responses to diversity), the communitarian rationale is grounded in promoting a sense of self-worth and a feeling of belonging—benefits to be had only through membership in a supportive community.

Two major problems confront the communitarian rationale. First, school choice advocates are not the first to have emphasized the importance of forging school communities, and choice is a more limited vehicle for doing so than they seem to believe. In a comprehensive school choice arrangement, many children will not get into their first-choice school; many others will wind up in schools by default. Even children who do get their first choice will be a widely diverse group. Thus choice cannot automatically forge community. Second, however much the communitarian rationale may differ from the market rationale in its underlying justification, where school choice is a self-standing reform that pays no attention to the necessity of taking other measures to insure that all children enjoy equality of educational opportunity, the market and communitarian rationales will yield the same effects.

The pragmatic rationale sees capitulating to some forms of school choice as required to save the public schools within the current political climate. More positively, it also sees school choice as a way to shake up an ossified and unresponsive school system. School choice plays quite a limited role in school reform on the pragmatic rationale in comparison with the other three. Rather than a "panacea," for instance, as Chubb and Moe (1990) would have it, school choice is an add-on that must be significantly circumscribed, particularly by the principle of equality of educational opportunity.

In the end, I embrace several forms of school choice that fit the pragmatic rationale, for example, means-tested vouchers and charter schools, but also recount several worries. First, the pragmatic rationale often goes under the name of "controlled choice," which, to my way of thinking, mistakenly puts the burden of proof on those who would do anything to limit choice and plays into the hands of the market rationale. "Meaningful choice" would help place the burden where it belongs. Second, the "slippery slope" poses a significant danger. Once school choice gets started, there may be no way of stopping it from completely eliminating the traditional democratic and egalitarian goals of the public schools.

In the concluding chapter, I review the (radical) liberal approach as well as its rationale. I suggest that it is defensible not only as a philosophical theory. Embedded as it is in our liberal-democratic traditions and vocabulary, it is also more likely to spur progressive educational change than are its contemporary competitors.

SITUATING THE ARGUMENTS

The arguments of this book fit squarely into the liberal tradition— at least into the *radical* strand exemplified by Dewey. Although providing an elaborate defense of this tradition against its many critics lies beyond my purposes, it is nonetheless useful to situate my project within the current conversation about educational justice. Thus I briefly consider liberalism in terms of four alternative political theories: communitarianism, postmodernism, critical theory, and feminism.

Communitarians identify liberalism with a conception of individuals as "radically unsituated" atoms, each pursuing his or her selfish interests (Sandel, 1982). Given liberalism, or so the argument goes, shared conceptions of good persons and good lives are precluded. As a consequence, ethical reasoning collapses into "emotivism"—a mere power struggle among individuals to satisfy their preferences (MacIntyre, 1981). Furthermore, lacking any grounds for agreement on what good persons and good lives are, the possibility of creating an "educated public"—a public that has some shared starting point and some shared standards for moral-political deliberation—is also precluded (MacIntyre, 1987).

Postmodernists take a different slant. They criticize liberalism for ignoring the tight connections between rationality and knowledge, on the one hand, and power, on the other. In this view, far from being neutral, the curriculum and instruction of liberal educational theory are rooted in the conceptions of rationality and knowledge of the dominant group, conceptions that are employed to marginalize and delegitimize other forms of rationality and knowledge by labeling them irrational and relativistic (e.g., Aronowitz & Giroux, 1991; Lather, 1991a).

Critical theorists have their roots in Marxism, which has historically criticized liberalism for ignoring the manner in which class membership underpins privilege and power (Bowles & Gintis, 1976, 1989). Finding traditional Marxist analysis too deterministic and simplistic, however, critical theorists have revised and extended it to include gender, race, culture, and ethnicity as sources of oppression (e.g., Apple, 1993a; Burbules, 1993; Young, 1990). These thinkers assign a significant role to economic class, but they also emphasize how gender, race, culture, and ethnicity interact with class to "distort" communication and disadvantage social groups vis-à-vis the dominant culture.

Feminism is much harder to portray than the preceding three perspectives, even if one uses the same kind of broad strokes. Feminists are united in the view that women are oppressed and in the commitment to end such oppression (Jaggar, 1983). Otherwise, feminism may be grounded in any of the above three perspectives, as well as in care theory or liberalism. The criticisms feminists advance against liberalism vary accordingly, ranging from dismissing it as untenable to calling for its revision.

Not surprisingly, the way in which liberals respond to their critics depends on the specific charge. In the case of communitarianism, liberals reject the picture it paints of the individual presupposed by liberalism as a caricature at best. Rawls (1971), for example, characterizes modern liberal society as a "union of social unions." Social unions have many of the characteristics that communitarians claim are missing from liberalism—close personal relationships and a shared history of values and practices, for example. At the societal level, these social unions are held together in a larger union by an "overlapping consensus" that puts general demands on them but that nonetheless permits maneuver space for community values to operate (Rawls, 1993). Given this conception, the individuals presupposed by liberalism do indeed need to be capable of sufficiently extricating themselves from particular personal relationships and social practices to assess the life situations in which they find themselves. They also need to be able to assess the kind of persons they wish to be. But engaging in and acting on this kind of reflection hardly require individuals to be "radically unsituated," to leave their former selves behind totally (Kymlicka, 1991; Rawls, 1993). Consider young women situated in a school community characterized by a significant degree of gender bias, for example. Aren't they capable of questioning the kind of identity that such a community foists upon them? And shouldn't they be empowered to initiate progressive change? Turning the table on communitarians, would it be better to insist that young women remain faithful to the norms and practices of such a community and to the identities it makes available?

The most general and often repeated response to postmodernism (not uniquely liberal) is that, to the extent that postmodernism is committed to ending oppression, it undermines its own mission. For if postmodernist reformers wish to totally conflate interests and power, on the one hand, with reason and knowledge, on the other—"deconstructing" liberty, equality, and justice in the process—then what possible grounds can there be for claiming that this or that group is (wrongly) oppressed? Can't the oppressed and their advocates be charged with merely asserting *their* interests? Benjamin Barber (1992) observes in this connection,

"Reason can be smoke screen for interest, but the argument that it is a smoke screen itself depends on reason" (p. 109).

My differences with critical theorists are considerably fewer than with communitarians or postmodernists. As it has evolved from traditional Marxism, critical theory has come to acknowledge the importance of individual agency. Meanwhile, as liberalism has evolved from libertarianism to more egalitarian forms, it has come to acknowledge the importance of economic structures in shaping the array of choices open to individuals as well as the importance of gender, race, culture, and ethnicity. Starting at different ends of the structure–agency continuum, then, the Marxist and liberal traditions have grown much closer to one another. Important differences still exist (my critical theorist colleagues and students inform me in no uncertain terms that they are Not liberals!), but these differences are typically not apparent when it comes to recommendations regarding educational policy and practice on the current U.S. scene.[8]

In the end, I am not convinced it matters much to quibble over whether the project of this book concedes too much to liberalism's critics to *really* be a liberal one.[9] What does matter is that I have fundamental differences with postmodernists and communitarians and fundamental affinities with (certain) feminists and critical theorists. In the chapters to follow, I freely appropriate—or largely ignore—various thinkers accordingly.

CHAPTER 2

A Radical Liberal Framework

*The natural distribution [of talents] is neither just nor unjust; nor is
it unjust that persons are born into society at some particular position. These are simply natural facts. What is just and unjust is the
way that institutions deal with these facts.*
                                        —*John Rawls*, A Theory of Justice

The concept of equal educational opportunity is a part of the conceptual
apparatus of liberal-democratic tradition, functioning within a network
of connected and mutually supporting concepts such as liberty, democracy, equality, choice, opportunity, and justice. In general, the liberal
democratic tradition is not strictly egalitarian, because its interpretation
of social justice does not require that the distribution of a society's goods
be equalized unconditionally. Instead, distributive equality is only a
prima facie requirement; distributive inequality is morally acceptable so
long as certain conditions are met, equal opportunity among them.

Equal *educational* opportunity occupies a pivotal place in this tradition. As I observed in Chapter 1, equality of educational opportunity is
now recognized as an essential requirement of equality of opportunity
more generally. Beyond this shared commitment, common to all forms
of liberal-democratic theory, however, vast differences exist among its
various strands regarding what equality of educational opportunity requires—differences that have profound implications for educational
policy.

In this chapter I sort out and evaluate these differences. I begin with
the equal opportunity versus equal results controversy, and challenge
what I call the "received view"—that there is a fundamental incoherence in identifying equality of educational opportunity with equality of
educational results. My aim here is to provide a clearer understanding
of the relationships between educational results, on the one hand, and
freedom, choice, and opportunities, on the other.

I then explicate the three predominant theories of justice in the
liberal-democratic tradition—libertarianism, utilitarianism, and liberal-

egalitarianism—paying particular attention to how each uses educational results to interpret equality of educational opportunity. I advance liberal-egalitarianism as the most adequate and proffer a "threshold"[1] interpretation of equality of educational opportunity. Such an interpretation requires equalizing certain educational results, within certain limits.

Finally, I round out the conceptual tool kit to be employed throughout the remainder of this book by dividing interpretations of equality of educational opportunity into three kinds: formal, compensatory, and participatory. These interpretations bear important relationships to the three theories of justice but do not straightforwardly map onto them. I advance the participatory interpretation as the most generally adequate. As its name perhaps suggests, it requires a major renegotiation of the aims and practices of schooling.

THE CRITERION OF EQUAL RESULTS: POLITICAL, NOT METAPHYSICAL[2]

Toward the end of her essay, "Opportunities, Equalities, and Education," Onora O'Neill (1976) remarks, "The concept of opportunity cannot be rid of its libertarian birthmark—even after radical surgery" (p. 292). She reaches this conclusion after rejecting James Coleman's (1968) claim that equal educational opportunity can be construed in terms of equal educational results. According to O'Neill, whatever its merits, equalizing educational results is fundamentally different from equalizing educational opportunity. She elaborates this view as follows:

> I know neither how to reconcile nor how to choose between an interpretation of the human condition as governed by natural laws and an interpretation of persons as autonomous choosers. . . . We are faced with the following alternatives. If persons are fundamentally autonomous choosers, their lives and activities should reflect their choices. They should not, and perhaps cannot be made equal in aspects of life, such as educational attainments, which reflect choices. A commitment to human equality in this case can be at most a commitment to equality of opportunity, that is to making the publicly controlled obstacles to activities and success equal. . . . If, on the other hand, persons are not fundamentally autonomous choosers, but the diverse products of diverse environments, then commitment to human equality must be more extensive. It must aim for more equal conditions of human life and cannot accept unequal results in significant areas, since these cannot be attributed to persons' varying private characteristics and are a concern of public policy. A commitment to equal education based on

this view must be more than a commitment to equal educational opportunity. (pp. 292–293)

Here O'Neill provides an explicit statement of the "received view,"[3] the central feature of which is a forced choice between two mutually exclusive interpretations of equality in education: an interpretation based on public control, determinism, and equal results and an interpretation based on private characteristics, freedom, and equal opportunities.

Compare O'Neill's perspective with the one advanced by Dewey (1922):

> [T]here are two schools of social reform. One bases itself upon the notion of a morality which springs from an inner freedom, something mysteriously cooped up within the personality. . . . The other school denies the existence of any such inner power, and in so doing conceives that it has denied all moral freedom. . . . There is an alternative to being penned in between these two theories. We can recognize that all conduct is interaction between elements of human nature and the environment, natural and social. Then we shall see that . . . freedom is found in the interaction which maintains an environment in which human desire and choice count for something. (pp. 309–310)

Dewey's "two schools of social reform" correspond to O'Neill's two interpretations of the human condition. Underlying the perception of being "penned in between these two theories" is a *metaphysical* sense of freedom, O'Neill's sense, quite removed from the political meaning that people ordinarily have in mind. For example, citizens could enjoy maximal freedom of movement, of expression, of religion, and of civil liberties in general; that is, they could enjoy maximal freedom in its ordinary political sense and still lack freedom in its metaphysical sense. For, unbeknownst to them, they might really be just highly complex automatons determined to behave as they do by various natural and social laws over which they have no control.

In typical pragmatic fashion, Dewey (1946, chap. 10) dismisses the "rigid conceptualism" he associates with this way of looking at things in favor of creating circumstances where ideas "count for something." In the process, he dismisses interpreting freedom in its metaphysical sense in favor of interpreting it in its political sense. He quips: "What men have esteemed and fought for in the name of liberty is varied and complex—but certainly it has never been a metaphysical freedom of the will" (1922, p. 303).

Dewey's approach thus forges a much closer link between metaphysics and politics than O'Neill's, but hers nonetheless has important political implications. In particular, identifying political freedom with metaphysical freedom construes freedom as wholly internal, such that fostering it consists merely in removing external impediments. Because more is required to provide freedom that "counts for something," construing freedom in this way is, as Daniel Dennett (1984) says, "politically retrograde." And where the principle of equality of educational opportunity is confined to removing external impediments, it, too, is politically retrograde. For just as freedom and choice should "count for something," so should opportunities.

Consider Dennett's (1984) notion of a "bare opportunity." He gives as an example the kind of opportunity prisoners have for escape when their jailer, unbeknownst to them because they are asleep, unlocks their cell doors for a short time during the night. What makes such an opportunity "bare" is that those who possess it are denied the information necessary ever to exercise it or even to know it exists. To take an example from education, students placed in vocational tracks who don't know, and whose parents don't know, the consequences of this kind of placement possess only a bare opportunity to attend the finest colleges. In general, because bare opportunities have no effect on how people choose to live their lives, they hardly seem to count for anything. Accordingly, they hardly seem "worth wanting."

In order for someone to possess a real opportunity, she or he must also possess certain relevant information, including, of course, the information that the opportunity exists. Furthermore, deliberation on the part of the person possessing a given opportunity must be effective in determining which among several possible outcomes is pursued. Consider the student deciding whether to choose between a vocational and a college preparatory track. Even if the pertinent information has been provided, a real opportunity will nonetheless fail to exist if the student does not know what to do with information because he or she lacks the capacity to deliberate. A real opportunity will also fail to exist if the student's deliberation is merely a sham because, owing to the judgment of the school counselors or to a shortage of available spots in the college preparatory track, for example, the vocational track is a fait accompli. Finally, a real opportunity will fail to exist if it is not within the person's power to bring about the chosen outcome. Consider once again the student deciding whether to pursue the vocational or college preparatory track. If the student is totally ill-equipped by prior schooling for the college preparatory track, then it would be misleading at best to say that the student has a real opportunity to succeed in this curriculum.

Of course, it is counterintuitive to suggest that in order for someone to have an opportunity for X, that person must be guaranteed to succeed at X. On the other hand, an opportunity merely to undergo X, when failure is virtually assured, is simply an opportunity to futilely try X and is no advance over a bare opportunity to X. Accordingly, such opportunities are neither real nor worth wanting. [Consider, e.g., a policy that putatively provides equal educational opportunities by providing students with "second chances" to try curricula for which they remain ill-prepared (House & Howe, 1990).] Thus, insofar as having an opportunity merely to undergo X does not constitute a real opportunity, a good chance of success (but not necessarily a guarantee) must be present in order for a real opportunity to exist.

But how good must the chance of success be? One fruitful way to address this question is to identify possible sources of the lack of power to bring about results. At least two such sources exist: uncertainty regarding desired results and unsupportive social and political conditions.

In order for deliberation and choice to have a point, uncertainty must exist regarding whether the desired results associated with a given choice will be realized and regarding what these results might be. For example, a student who resolves to attend Harvard will have to cope with the possibility that he or she may ultimately fail to qualify, qualify but have insufficient income, qualify but have to decline because of the death of a parent, and so forth. Presumably, these sorts of considerations will have entered into the student's deliberation. Furthermore, and to complicate matters significantly, the student is also likely to be uncertain about what the less immediate, hoped for results of completing Harvard might be, such as a good job and a high income. These kinds of uncertainty constitute both an obstacle to individuals' power to bring about the desired results of their choices and a reason an opportunity is not a guarantee of results. Moreover, these kinds of uncertainty cannot be altogether eliminated and can thwart the results individuals seek with their choices. The existence of uncertainty, however, is consistent with eliminating raw contingency in individuals' lives to the extent possible. As Rawls (1971) observes in this vein, "The social system is not an unchangeable order beyond human control but a pattern of human action" (p. 102).

The existence of a (real) opportunity, then, requires a favorable *context of choice*,[4] in which the thwarting of the desired results of individuals' choices is reduced as far as possible to the kind of uncertainty that gives *deliberation* and *choice* their meanings. This, in turn, requires that certain results obtain. For example, "X has been provided an opportunity to attend Harvard," entails that X has sufficient income, talent, and so forth, and that X has the information and skill needed to deliberate effectively about whether to attend. If X doesn't have the income or talent, then X lacks an opportunity in a rather straightforward way; if X lacks information or skill in deliberation, then X has only a "bare" opportunity. An important corollary is that educational opportunity is *treelike* with respect to educational results. For example, if a given result, such as literacy, fails to obtain by a certain point in an individual's educational career, then the range of educational *opportunity branches* subsequently open to such an individual will be significantly pruned.

This analysis of the concept of educational opportunity carries over straightforwardly into the interpretation of *equality* of educational opportunity. Against the received view that equalizing educational opportunity and equalizing educational results are fundamentally different, interpretations of equality of educational opportunity may be placed on a continuum of political stances that differ in the degree to which they sanction intervening in the social system to minimize fortuitousness in individuals' lives. Construed in this way, interpretations of equality of educational opportunity are distinguished simply in terms of how committed they are to intervening in the social system to equalize the conditions required to engender real educational opportunities. This turns the received view on its head. Rather than equalizing educational results, it is equalizing (bare) opportunities that cannot count as an interpretation of the principle of equality of educational opportunity.

The relationship between educational results and equality of educational opportunity can be more fully elaborated in terms of a certain version of the received view developed by Nicholas Burbules and Ann Sherman (1979). Like all proponents of the received view, Burbules and Sherman claim that equal educational results is not a possible interpretation of equal educational opportunity. But, refining the way of dividing things up, they distinguish two interpretations of equal educational opportunity: "formalist" and "actualist." Formalist interpretations are minimalist, requiring only the absence of formal barriers to access. Actualist interpretations go beyond formalist, requiring intervention to mitigate disadvantages.

In its purest form, a formalist interpretation would have as its only constraint equality under the law, such that no legal impediments prevent whoever chooses to from attending private schools, residing in the best school districts, and so forth. But it is difficult to see how this most minimalist interpretation can be construed as an interpretation of equality of educational opportunity, for it provides only the barest of bare educational opportunities to many children. It is rooted in unfettered liberty rather than in equality of educational opportunity.

Thus formalist interpretations shade into equal access [or equal "inputs" (Coleman, 1968)] interpretations, in which equalizing educational opportunity requires equalizing features of access—library holdings, quality of teachers, physical facilities, and so forth. But, as Coleman (1968) astutely observes, such equal access interpretations cannot float entirely free of the criterion of educational results, because it is impossible to determine what counts as a feature of access without knowing or conjecturing how it is related to educational results—does the appearance of a school's lawn count? the mean age of its teachers? the number of drinking fountains? Given the equal access version of the formalist interpretation, then, unequal educational results serve to flag the possibility of unequal features of access. Equal results would presumably indicate that equality of educational opportunity exists.

Formalist interpretations either render educational results irrelevant, at the cost of not being interpretations of equality of educational opportunity at all, or collapse into some sort of results-based view. Insofar as formalist views do have something to do with educational results, they simply have rather lax standards for equality. For instance, systematic inequality of results among income groups does not entail inequality of opportunity provided that access (however that is defined) is equal; opportunity would be unequal only if, say, the low-income schools were opened fewer hours or had a demonstrably inferior teaching corps. This simply boils down to the view that low income and its associated effects are not relevant to the question of whether educational opportunity is equal. Such a view fails to require anything close to (real) educational opportunities.

Actualist interpretations come closer to requiring (real) educational opportunities by demanding that systematic differences in educational results among groups be subjected to closer scrutiny. In particular, unlike formal interpretations, which confine themselves to the features of schools, actualist interpretations take seriously how these features interact with the characteristics of students. For example, low income is one of the first factors that actualist interpretations would consider an illegitimate cause of unequal results. Talent, too, would be ruled out by more egalitarian versions. In the limiting case (i.e., the most egalitarian and interventionist version), the only legitimate source of unequal results permitted under an actualist interpretation would be *choosing* to forego an opportunity.

Actualist interpretations clearly make substantial use of the criterion of educational results and are therefore results-based in an important sense. Indeed, it is difficult to see how actualist interpretations can really occupy a middle ground between formal and equal-results interpretations. For the appeal to the exercise of choice, ultimately the

only way to draw the line between actualist and equal-results interpretations, turns out to be an inadequate criterion (Green, 1991). Some
choices may be legitimately overridden, even when made by otherwise
autonomous adults—consider the choice to have racially segregated
schools. Other choices may be overridden because of a lack of delibera-
tive capacity or relevant information on the part of choice makers—
consider the educational choices of children. Finally, the mere fact that
an individual affirms a choice does not mean that freedom and opportunities worth wanting exist—consider the impoverished student who
chooses a vocational rather than a college preparatory curriculum in
hopes of soon being able to earn an income.

Precisely what educational results are adopted as the criterion of
equality of educational opportunity is an important consideration, as are
the means by which they may be pursued. Results-based interpretations
appear both incoherent and threatening when they are conjoined with a
certain model of the relationship between educational means and ends.
This model portrays equal-results interpretations as adopting some educational end (say, compliance with school rules) and then employing
whatever means (say, drugs) that may yield it. Equal educational results
as the criterion of equality of educational opportunity is then criticized
as being incoherent, as well as morally repugnant, because no choice
need be exercised on the part of students and because the means need
not be ''educational'' (Burbules, 1990).

This model makes some questionable assumptions. In particular,
when the overarching educational end is identified with freedom (worth
wanting), intermediate educational results must be judged in terms of
the role they play in attaining it. Thus the end of freedom constrains
legitimate means. The social world and the individuals within it, after
all, are fundamentally unpredictable, and this gives freedom, opportunity, dignity, and a host of other concepts that make up our moral
perspective their significance. This also explains why means such as
indoctrination and coercion, for instance, are objectionable: They cannot
work to foster the desired end of freedom (Howe, 1990).

EQUALITY OF EDUCATIONAL RESULTS, EQUALITY OF EDUCATIONAL OPPORTUNITY, AND LIBERAL THEORIES OF JUSTICE

An interpretation of equality of educational opportunity may be evaluated properly only within the broader theory of distributive justice in
which it finds its home. For it is such a theory that determines the kinds

of educational results to target and the extent to which they should be equalized. In this section I examine three theories of distributive justice within the liberal democratic tradition—libertarianism, utilitarianism, and liberal-egalitarianism. How they treat the criterion of educational results is my central concern. Briefly, libertarianism eschews results as virtually irrelevant; utilitarianism views results as relevant but does not require that they be equal; and liberal-egalitarianism requires that at least *some* results be equal. I aim to show that libertarianism and utilitarianism are hopelessly flawed, and that only liberal-egalitarianism provides a general account of equality of educational opportunity consistent with the demands of justice in a liberal democracy.

Libertarianism

Libertarians object in principle to the redistribution of goods by governments, an objection that applies to utilitarianism and liberal-egalitarianism alike.[5] For libertarians, individual liberty is the overriding value; only a "minimalist" state can be justified—a state whose power is restricted to protecting its citizens' rights to be free from crime, foreign belligerents, interference in executing contracts, and the like. In particular, unequal patterns of results cannot be used to justify taking certain individuals' resources in order to promote the welfare of others.

The principle of equality of educational opportunity thus take on a somewhat unconventional meaning and function in libertarian theory. Respect for equality is respect for liberty, and the function of equality of educational opportunity (if this is a useful libertarian concept at all) is not to equalize results but to insure that individuals (or their parents) are free to pursue any form of education they freely choose.

What most clearly divides libertarian thinkers like Nozick (1974) from more egalitarian thinkers like Rawls is their respective attitudes about natural and social contingencies. For Rawls (1971), individuals can be neither credited nor blamed for the attributes they draw in the "natural lottery"—intelligence, talents, and health, for example—and a just society will attempt to level the inevitable inequality in results for which individuals are not responsible. For Nozick, although the natural lottery might be *unfortunate* for certain individuals, it is not thereby *unfair*; individuals are "entitled" to whatever characteristics they draw in the natural lottery and to whatever flows from these characteristics. Distributions of goods that result from free exchanges among consenting adults are just, according to Nozick, no matter how unequal the resulting distribution and despite the fact that certain individuals start life with significant advantages.

Perhaps the most puzzling aspect of libertarian theory is how oblivious it seems to the ineluctable notion of social causation—a notion underpinning social science and impossible to ignore, given today's understanding of the workings of modern societies. The suggestion that patterns of results should be explicated in terms of a history of choices and bargains, and that the patterns are just where coercion (in its more obvious and blatant forms) is absent, is tenuous at best. Coercion can be subtle and choices can be constrained. The notion that being born into poverty, for instance, has no effect on one's life chances, that society has no responsibility for ameliorating this circumstance, that this is "unfortunate but not unfair" and all that is required of the unlucky person is an exercise of will, is beyond the pale.

Libertarians like Nozick would, of course, concede that conditions of poverty can be unjust—provided they pass a very strict test. Such conditions must result demonstrably from a history of unjust "transfers"—as in the case of slavery, for instance—not from the effects of social determination, such that inequality of results constitutes good evidence of inequality of opportunity. But how is libertarian theory to be used to guide the formulation of practical policy? For example, there is little question that African Americans still suffer the effects of slavery and that the transfer of vast regions of North America from Native Americans to European immigrants was unjust. Is the solution to trace the histories of the transfers for each individual and to "rectify" all those deemed unjust? This seems a horribly complex, indeed impossible, task.

The problems do not end here. Even if by some miracle everything could be put right, gross inequalities would arise again in no time. For example, children whose parents made bad deals, succumbed to drugs, deserted them, and so forth, would be put at a severe disadvantage because of the bad choices of their parents. Perhaps a libertarian's obvious response is an appeal to the principle of merit as the means by which to distribute educational opportunities. But this response raises at least two serious problems. First, the likelihood that a child will become academically meritorious is determined by how that child has fared in the "lottery." Thus the questions of determining the history of transfers and mitigating bad parental choices arise anew. Second, it is by no means obvious that the appeal to merit is theoretically consistent. Because libertarianism is based on free-market/free-contract principles, parents would seem free to distribute educational opportunities on the basis of any criterion to which they freely agree, including ability to pay. It follows that if merit is to serve as the criterion for distributing educational opportunities, then libertarians must incorporate an additional principle that limits the kinds of agreements that can be struck. There is thus no way to sanction any plausible principle of distribution without moving beyond the confines of libertarian political theory.

Utilitarianism

Utilitarianism is notorious for the number of interpretations to which it is open, and I focus on the one I find most pertinent to the issue of equal educational opportunity: "meritocratic utilitarianism." This is the basic framework Strike (1984) uses to characterize the view expressed in *A Nation at Risk* (1983), and it is made up of two principles: (a) Educational policies are to be evaluated on the basis of their effects on economic productivity, and (b) educational opportunities are to be distributed (and designed) on the basis of economically valuable skills.

A program like Head Start, for example, could be justified on the grounds that it promotes equality of educational opportunity by distributing opportunities on the basis of economically valuable skills, "merit." Because such economically valuable skills would otherwise go undetected and undeveloped, such a program for the disadvantaged also maximizes productivity. Meritocratic utilitarianism has no difficulty with the notion that government ought to distribute resources in order to achieve desirable results—indeed, that is the major aim of the theory—and equality of educational opportunity is simply one potential device for promoting this aim. Thus, unlike libertarianism, utilitarianism has no built-in hostility toward incorporating results into its interpretation of equality of educational opportunity.

On the other hand, equality of educational opportunity suffers a precarious existence within meritocratic utilitarianism, because it is held hostage to maximizing productivity and because a set of conditions under which maximizing productivity would conflict with equalizing educational results is easy to imagine. Consider again the example of Head Start. Suppose the children enrolled are faring better than they otherwise would—educational results are being equalized—but that a cost-benefit analysis reveals economic productivity would be enhanced if the resources devoted to Head Start were spent on scientific and technical education for children talented in these fields. Under these conditions, equalizing educational results would not be sanctioned by meritocratic utilitarianism. On the contrary, the theory would dictate instead that the resources go to scientific and technical education and, as a consequence, that educational results become even less equal.[6]

Unlike libertarianism, then, utilitarianism is congenial to incorporating results into its interpretation of equal educational opportunity;

but, like libertarianism, it provides no principled way to insure that opportunities will indeed be equalized. Equality of educational opportunity is rendered secondary to maximizing the good, which is often identified with maximizing economic productivity. Utilitarianism thus also fails to provide an adequate foundation on which to ground the principle of equality of educational opportunity.

Liberal-Egalitarianism

The shortcomings of libertarianism and utilitarianism point to the alternative—liberal-egalitarianism. I apply this label indifferently to liberal views that limit the kinds of distributions of society's goods that are permissible more strictly than do their libertarian and utilitarian counterparts.[7]

Various candidate principles have been put forward to serve this role, and John Rawls's (1971) "difference principle"—always distribute so as to most improve the situation of the least advantaged—is no doubt the most celebrated. In my view, so-called threshold principles have the most to offer when it comes to the distribution of education, but this is not the place to develop a defense of this claim.[8] Liberal-egalitarian distributive principles share enough in their underlying justification to make such a defense an unnecessary distraction.

I call my particular version of the educational threshold the "participatory educational ideal" and have more to say about its substantive content in subsequent chapters (particularly the next two, on gender and multiculturalism, respectively). For the time being, I retain the threshold language and limit myself to four of its general features.

First, the threshold is an individual good. Because educational attainment is linked to other goods such as income, employment, and health, a certain level is required to enable individuals to lead a decent and rewarding life.

Second, the threshold is a collective good. Because of both the role it plays in relation to other social goods and the role it plays (or could play) more directly, a state characterized by massive inequality in the distribution of education is also characterized by massive inequality in its citizens' political effectiveness. Such a state can be democratic in name only.

Third, the threshold is needs-based. Because different individuals require different amounts of educational effort and resources to achieve the threshold, effort and resources must be distributed differentially.

Fourth, the threshold is results-based in the way described in the preceding section. It falls toward the interventionist end of the continuum of interpretations of equality of educational opportunity. But, as distinct from a strict form of egalitarianism, it limits the requirement to equalize educational results. Individuals are different, and choices accumulate. Even under conditions of (real) equality of educational opportunity, the treelike feature of educational careers opens certain avenues of endeavor and closes others. Accordingly, not all educational goals and activities are to be associated with what the threshold requires, and, where they are not, individual and community choice should be free to operate. Although the threshold limits the principles of both liberty and utility, it eliminates neither.

THE PARTICIPATORY INTERPRETATION OF EQUALITY OF EDUCATIONAL OPPORTUNITY AND THE CRITERION OF EQUAL EDUCATIONAL WORTH

Liberal-egalitarianism is typically construed as a compensatory view.[9] That is, society's goods, including education, are presumed uncontroversial, and compensatory measures (programs like Head Start, for instance) are instituted that render the competition for such goods more fair. An increasingly heard criticism of compensatory views is that because they take societal goods as given, they merely reinforce the status quo and marginalize groups who have had no part in formulating it. This criticism has merit, and it may be applied straightforwardly to interpretations of equality of educational opportunity.

In this section I describe a compensatory interpretation of equality of educational opportunity more fully and examine it in light of the above criticism. I then introduce a ''participatory'' interpretation as a way to meet this criticism that requires abandoning neither the principle of equality of educational opportunity nor liberal-egalitarianism. The basic idea behind the participatory interpretation is that genuine equality of educational opportunity can frequently be achieved only by including the voices of groups who have historically been excluded in negotiating what educational opportunities have worth. But first, for completeness, I briefly revisit and expand my discussion of the formal interpretation.

The Formal Interpretation Revisited

The formal interpretation, again, identifies equality of educational opportunity with the formal structure of educational institutions. In its purest form, it requires only the absence of formal barriers to participation based on morally irrelevant criteria such as race and gender. In a slightly stronger form, it also requires equalizing resources among schools, at least up to some floor. The formal interpretation can serve a progressive function, for banning legally sanctioned racial barriers to educational opportunity was surely a moral advance, and removing such barriers for children with disabilities and for females was an advance as well. Furthermore, areas still remain in which achieving even formal equality of educational opportunity would be a vast improvement over the present situation—in school finance, for example (Kozol, 1991).

For the most part, however, the formal interpretation falls considerably short of the goal to which the principle of equal educational opportunity should aspire. It is far too often insensitive to the profound influence that social factors can have on educational opportunities, even when formal barriers are absent and resources such as funding are equalized. For example, the educational opportunities of a monolingual Chinese-speaking child in classes conducted exclusively in English are hardly equal to those of a monolingual English-speaking classmate. And this is precisely what the Supreme Court decided in the celebrated *Lau v. Nichols* (1974) case when it declared that the educational opportunities provided to Chinese children under these circumstances were not "meaningful."

In order, then, for educational opportunities to be meaningful—to be worth wanting—they cannot be construed in terms of the formal features of educational institutions alone. Again, they must be construed in terms of the interaction between these features and the characteristics that individuals bring to educational institutions. It follows that the ideal of equality of educational opportunity should not be identified with a formal *system of equal educational opportunities*—defined in terms of the features of educational institutions—but with *a system of educational opportunities of equal worth*—defined in terms of the interaction between individuals and educational institutions.

The Compensatory Interpretation

In contrast to the formal interpretation, the compensatory interpretation is sensitive to the importance of how interactions between the characteristics of individuals and the features of educational institutions can function to increase or diminish the worth of formal educational opportunities. The compensatory interpretation is also sensitive to the observation that if educational opportunities are to have worth, they must be conceived in terms of educational careers rather than in terms of specific (formal) opportunities abstracted from such careers. The goal is to help shape desirable educational careers by compensating for characteristics of individuals that disadvantage them in educational institutions. For example, bilingual education is a means by which to compensate for the language disadvantage of non-English-speaking children; special education is a means by which to compensate for disabilities; Head Start is a means by which to compensate for economic disadvantages; and so forth. The general objective in each case is to provide children with the special or missing educational opportunities that will expand and enhance the worth of their educational careers.

The compensatory interpretation is prominent both in liberal political theory and in educational policy. It is the general kind of interpretation typically associated with both utilitarianism and liberal-egalitarianism, and it underlies much federal law as well (Salamone, 1986). It has also become a target of increasing criticism, from the right as well as from the left.

Rightists include libertarians and conservative moralists who, although they differ markedly in their view of civil liberties, both criticize the compensatory interpretation because of the governmental intervention it requires and because of the way in which it putatively places far too little emphasis on individual initiative and responsibility. Rightists are associated with a formalist interpretation of equality of educational opportunity, and I have nothing to add at this point by way of criticism. (In subsequent chapters, I evaluate formal interpretations further in the context of specific educational policies and practices.) More germane here are critics from the left.

As I mentioned in Chapter 1, leftists have historically criticized the compensatory interpretation for being insensitive to sources of inequality that are found in underlying economic structures, particularly as related to social class (Bowles & Gintis, 1976, 1989). Although these critics would likely concede that a compensatory interpretation is generally preferable to a formal interpretation, they are highly critical of both, indeed, of the principle of equality of educational opportunity per se. Focusing on equalizing educational opportunity diverts attention from the underlying structural sources of inequality associated with social class and, in the process, serves to legitimate and perpetuate vast inequality.

As I also mentioned, over the last several decades liberal political theory has come under increasing criticism for insensitivity to the effects of race and gender in addition to the effects of class (e.g., McCarthy, 1993). Critics point to how the various and overlapping disparities that exist in educational opportunities and achievement among girls versus

boys, men versus women, and minority cultures versus White culture
are inconsistent with a commitment to equality. Where these kinds of
disparities are the basis for calls to achieve much greater equality across
groups by equalizing educational opportunities, they do not fundamentally challenge the principle of equality of educational opportunity. Instead, they demand that it to live up to its promise.

There is a deeper form of criticism, however, that not only goes
beyond but is often at odds with the kind just described. As Janet Radcliff Richards (1980) observes, "If a group is kept out of doing something
long enough, it is overwhelmingly likely that activities . . . will develop
in a way unsuited to the excluded group" (pp. 113–114). In this vein,
current liberal society is characterized as being through and through
a product and reflection of the historical dominance of White males,
particularly those possessing economic power. Although various critics
can substantially disagree, they all seem to converge on the following
general conclusion: The liberal quest for equality is a sham because it
serves merely to ensconce the status quo, rendering White males the
standard of comparison and requiring disempowered groups to play by
rules they had no part in formulating and whose interests such rules do
not serve.

In the case of women, various scholars maintain that certain ways
of thinking and relating to others, as well as certain interests, are peculiar to women's experience (e.g., Belenky, Clinchy, Goldberger, & Tarule, 1986; Gilligan, 1982; Noddings, 1984), but that an appreciation of
these differences is rarely reflected in society's institutions (e.g., Noddings, 1990; Okin, 1989; Salamone, 1986). For its part, the educational
system in particular tends implicitly to embrace the gendered attitudes
and practices of society at large and to respond to and sort girls and
women accordingly, in their roles both as educators and students (e.g.,
Apple, 1988; Martin, 1994; Oakes, 1990; Sadker & Sadker, 1994; Weiler,
1988). Moreover, women are faced with a "double bind" insofar as they
must pay a price when they *do* play by the existing rules. For certain
traits are "genderized," so that women are judged differently from men
for exhibiting what otherwise seems to be the same behavior (Martin,
1982).

Similar problems confront people of color. Castelike minorities—
minorities that have involuntarily become a part of the political-
economic system—are faced with the dilemma of either playing by the
rules of the dominant culture and compromising their cultural identity
or refusing to play and paying a price for preserving it (Ogbu & Matute-
Bianchi, 1986). African Americans, for instance, can either embrace the
practice of "acting White" to succeed in school or adopt an "oppositional" stance that often dooms them to poor performance (Fordham,

1993; Ogbu, 1992). A related set of problems faces indigenous peoples such as North American aboriginals (Kymlicka, 1991).

In summary, the compensatory interpretation has the advantage over the formal interpretation of acknowledging and seeking to mitigate individual and social factors that operate to disadvantage certain groups in educational institutions. However, it is vulnerable to the criticism that it implicitly adopts the status quo regarding what is of educational worth and how this is to be determined. It therefore fails to afford educational opportunities of equal worth to individuals who have had no part in shaping the educational practices and curricular content that are deemed educationally worthwhile.

The Participatory Interpretation

One response to this challenge is to abandon the principle of equality of educational opportunity as a principle that inherently and irremediably legitimates dominance. Of late, several liberal-egalitarian theorists have marshaled a second response (Kymlicka, 1990, 1991; Okin, 1989). These theorists concede that the liberal tradition historically has been insensitive to the importance of factors such as culture and gender, and that such insensitivity does indeed render it vulnerable to the charge of legitimating domination. Rather than abandoning liberalism, however, these theorists call for a rethinking of what liberal principles demand, particularly the principle of equality.

Will Kymlicka (1991), for instance, contends that an adequate interpretation of equality is implicit in the work of seminal liberal thinkers such as Rawls and Dworkin, even if they do not themselves articulate it adequately. In particular, Kymlicka contends that Rawls's (1971) inclusion of "self-respect" among the "primary goods" that society must justly distribute opens the door to—indeed, requires—including a place for the effective expression and incorporation of cultural and gendered identities in the design of society's institutions. This is so because maintaining one's group identity, and having what flows from it respected and taken seriously, is inextricably bound up with self-respect. In this general vein, Kymlicka (1991) observes,

> [I]t only makes sense to invite people to participate in politics (or for people to accept that invitation) if they are treated as equals. . . . And that is incompatible with defining people in terms of roles they did not shape or endorse. (p. 89)

The kind of view Kymlicka represents thus takes very seriously the objection that mere differential treatment in the name of responding to special needs, interests, and capabilities—mere compensation for disadvantages—is insufficient or objectionable if it is not also rooted in equal respect for different views on what worthwhile needs, interests, and capabilities are, particularly when self-identity and self-respect are at stake. Iris Marion Young (1990b, chap. 7) echoes and extends this view:

> Groups with different circumstances or forms of life should be able to participate together in public institutions without shedding their distinct identities or suffering disadvantage because of them. The goal is not to give special compensation to the deviant until they achieve normality, but rather to denormalize the way institutions formulate their rules by revealing the plural circumstances and needs that exist, or ought to exist, within them. (p. 134)

If we apply these observations to education, educational institutions, too, need "to denormalize the way [they] formulate their rules by revealing the plural circumstances and needs that exist, or ought to exist, within them." In terms of the principle of equality of educational opportunity, a participatory interpretation is required.

In subsequent chapters I illustrate, test, and further refine the participatory interpretation. In the next two, on gender and multiculturalism, respectively, I give special attention to a particularly difficult challenge it faces. Specifically, although it reorients the discussion in a way that promises to overcome several difficulties that plague the principle of equality of educational opportunity, it does not manage to avoid the problem, central to liberal educational theory, of mandating some uniform educational ideal for all students who attend public schools. On the contrary, the participatory interpretation exacerbates the problem because it opens the ideal to negotiation, whereas formal and compensatory interpretations take the ideal for granted.

CONCLUSION

Having and exercising an educational opportunity can be understood only within a context of choice, the features of which are determined by the interaction between individuals and social conditions. The manner in which educational institutions manipulate these interactions to achieve educational results significantly shapes the educational careers that individuals experience. Which educational results to produce, and to what extent they should be equalized, is determined by a theory of justice. Among liberal theories, libertarianism is inadequate because of the hollow kind of equality of educational opportunity it implies. Utilitarianism is inadequate because it has no principled way to protect equality of educational opportunity adequately. Only liberal-egalitarianism provides a liberal theory of justice from which an adequate interpretation of equality of educational opportunity can be derived.

Liberal-egalitarianism has historically been associated with a compensatory interpretation of equality of educational opportunity. Such an interpretation acknowledges the interactive nature of contexts of choice and seeks to remove disadvantages. But it is inadequate in many circumstances because it preempts debate about what is to be deemed educationally worthwhile by wrongly accepting as satisfactory the standards and practices associated with the status quo, in terms of which the marginalized and excluded should be compensated. In response, liberal-egalitarianism has moved toward participatory interpretations that seek to avoid the inadequacies of both compensatory and formal interpretations by including in the articulation of equal educational opportunity the need to question and negotiate what the educational standards and practices worth wanting should be.

The participatory interpretation provides a potential means of responding to some fundamental challenges to the ideal of equality of educational opportunity. A successful response must show that this ideal need not be jettisoned as unworkable or irremediably inegalitarian. And a very good reason not to jettison it is the prominent place it continues to occupy in the thinking of teachers and administrators as well as that of citizens, policy makers, and social researchers. Joining this conversation and moving it in the right direction has the best chance of success if, rather than prodding people to give up their deeply held principles, it prods them to reflect upon and consequently live up to what these principles demand.[10]

CHAPTER 3

Gender

Men's physiology defines most sports, their needs define auto and health insurance, their socially-designed biographies define workplace expectations and successful career patterns, their perspectives and concerns define quality in scholarship, their experiences and obsessions define merit, their objectification of life defines art, their military service defines citizenship, their presence defines family, their inability to get along with one another—their wars and rulerships—defines history, their image defines god, and their genitals define sex. For each of their differences from women, what amounts to an affirmative action plan is in effect, otherwise known as the structure and values of American society.

—*Catharine MacKinnon*, Feminism Unmodified

However one responds to MacKinnon's scathing assessment of the current scene vis-à-vis gender equality, there is no denying that, when results are taken as the indicator, the opportunities available to men and women in the United States vastly differ—and vastly favor men. As of mid-1996, 2 members of the Supreme Court, 48 members of the House of Representatives, and 6 members of the Senate are women; and these meager numbers are all-time highs. In employment, men hold a disproportionate number of high-paying positions, and they receive higher pay for the same positions, even when factors such as marital status are eliminated as possible causes of disparities (Adelman, 1991). In the family, where married men and women both work outside the home, women assume a disproportionate share of the responsibility for child-rearing and housework. In the event of divorce, men benefit financially, whereas women suffer (Okin, 1989).

Educational statistics are somewhat mixed. For example, girls and women consistently match or exceed the performance of boys and men at all levels of education (as measured by grades and class standing), and girls and women are gaining increasing access to math, science, and professional education (Adelman, 1991; Eccles, 1989; Linn & Petersen,

1985; Oakes, 1990). Overall, however, the statistics on education are only marginally better than those associated with government, employment, and the family. In the 1990s girls continue to score lower on standardized tests of achievement and to experience classrooms and curricula that are hostile to their interests and modes of interaction (American Association of University Women [AAUW], 1991, 1993; Riordan, 1990). Particularly in high school, many more girls than boys are eliminated from the educational "pipeline," which leads to an underrepresentation of women in science and engineering at the college level (Brush, 1991; Oakes, 1990). High school also seems to be a place where many girls adopt the "culture of romance," which leads them to abandon their educational and career goals in college (Holland & Eisenhart, 1990). The makeup of the teaching corps, administrations, and school boards is also lopsided. Overall, 72% of teachers are women, whereas 72% of principals and 95% of superintendents are men (Klein & Ortman, 1994).

TWO APOLOGIES FOR GENDER INEQUALITY

These patterns of inequality beg for a remedy. Or do they? I begin by entertaining two apologies for gender inequality that purportedly render these patterns morally legitimate: human nature and freedom of choice.

The Argument from Human Nature

Based on his view of the nature of women, a view no doubt widely shared in his time, Rousseau (as cited in Gutmann, 1987) claimed "the duties of women at all times [that] ought to be taught from childhood" are

> to please men, to be useful to them, to make herself loved and honored by them, to raise them when young, to care for them when grown, to counsel them, to console them, to make their lives agreeable and sweet. (p. 126)

In light of the burgeoning membership of groups such as the Promise Keepers and recent events such as the Million Man March, Rousseau's view is apparently still widely held. This is so in spite of John Stuart Mill's (1869/1992) simple, though no less telling, criticism of this view advanced over a century ago: "If women have a greater inclination for some things than others, there is no need for laws or social inculcation to make the majority of them do the former in preference to the latter" (p. 282). In the name of what is natural, it makes little more sense now to argue that we should not change traditional social arrangements vis-à-vis women than it did at an earlier point in history to argue that we should not change traditional social arrangements vis-à-vis slaves. (Of course, slavery was once defended as natural, too, and this should tell us something.)

No doubt certain "natural" physiological differences exist between the sexes that cannot be changed (at least for the time being), but translating these differences into differences in social roles and responsibilities requires some rather large leaps in inference, particularly in today's technological society. Characteristics such as physical strength, for example, are themselves an outgrowth of the "politics of the body" (Connell, 1987) and have come to be much less salient in modern industrial societies. In addition to its effects on paid work, technology has so changed domestic work, as well as childbirth and childrearing, that strictly physiological characteristics are rarely relevant to the social activities individuals are capable of performing. When physiological characteristics are relevant, as in the case of the capacity to become pregnant and give birth, for instance, their effects can be mitigated by instituting practices such as universal access to free child care and parental leaves for both men and women.

Of course, the argument from natural gender differences need not rest its case on physiological differences between the sexes. It can appeal to "natural" psychological differences instead. Although such psychological differences might have underlying physiological causes, understanding and explaining psychological differences in terms of physiology is not generally seen as necessary. All that seems to be required is that the psychological differences in question be pervasive and stable. Historically, support for differences has been found largely in folk psychology and religion. Only recently has empirical research begun to explore these differences as more than an afterthought.

The findings of this research go in different directions. One line of research supports the conclusion that differences in academic achievement associated with gender are minimal and can be eliminated with appropriate kinds of teaching (Feingold, 1988; Linn & Petersen, 1985; Linn & Hyde, 1989; Oakes, 1990; Eccles, 1989). But another line of research supports the conclusion that pervasive and stable gender differences do exist with respect to interests, attitudes, "ways of knowing," and modes of social interaction (Belenky et al., 1986; Gilligan, 1982).

But even if the existence of pervasive and stable gender differences is granted, they do not ipso facto count in favor of preserving the status quo. On the one hand, the mere presence of certain psychological tend-encies within a group is insufficient to justify particular social arrange-ments that complement and reinforce those tendencies, for this obvi-ously neglects the role that social practices play in shaping psychological tendencies of groups—social practices that may be responsible for caus-ing the very tendencies that are putatively natural and that putatively cause the social practices.[1] (Consider discouraging girls from pursuing a career in science on the grounds that they are naturally suited for caring roles such as elementary teaching or nursing because these occupations are almost the exclusive province of women.) On the other hand, even if women do speak with a different voice in some more purely natural sense, it does not follow that the status quo ought to be preserved, unless women use their different voice to support leaving things as they are (Houston, 1988). And a significant number do not.

Gender Inequality as Chosen

The alternative suggestion that girls and women have chosen the pres-ent arrangements is the kind of justification characteristic of libertarian-ism and its formalist interpretation of the principle of equality of oppor-tunity. Libertarians can make this suggestion with a straight face because they require so little evidence regarding what counts as free choice. That is, in the absence of evidence to the contrary, libertarians assume that choices are freely made. Accordingly, the burden of prov-ing that existing inequalities are the result of something other than freely made choices falls on those who claim that girls and women are denied equality of educational opportunity.

I argued in Chapter 2 for dismissing the libertarian conception of choice wholesale, on the grounds that it provides an insufficiently com-plex and robust account of the context of choice. The example of school-girls' curricular choices provides a compelling case in point. I focus particularly on their choices regarding math and science education, the portion of the curriculum studied most heavily by far.

Jeannie Oakes (1990) provides a comprehensive review of the em-pirical research regarding the relationships among girls' opportunities, choices, and achievement with respect to math and science curricula. She suggestively interprets much of what research reveals in terms of a "scientific pipeline" from which boys and girls are included or excluded over the course of their educational careers. In general, girls and boys do not differ notably at the elementary level, but girls are then win-nowed from math and science as they move through the higher grades. At the middle and junior high school level, girls and boys achieve equally, but girls start to display a more negative attitude and begin to go "underground" (Gilligan, 1991). At the senior high school level, girls' negativity increases, and they display less confidence in their math and science ability as well as in their academic ability in general. Furthermore, their achievement drops and they elect fewer advanced math and science courses than boys do, which is a major cause of girls' leaving the pipeline (Eccles, 1989).

In the end, then, girls do *choose* to leave the pipeline. But these choices must be viewed in terms of the larger context of choice, the cumulative effects of which are quite powerful in encouraging them to leave. Setting aside the effects of the family and the broader society, Oakes (1990) identifies three general features of schools that squeeze girls out of the pipeline. First, teachers hold expectations and employ teaching strategies and activities that systematically favor boys over girls. In particular, teachers have higher expectations for boys in math and science, interact with them more, and use predominantly competitive/whole-group instructional methods. Second, girls receive less encouragement to pursue careers in math and science and less advice about how to go about it. This happens directly, through the words and deeds of teachers and counselors, and indirectly, through role modeling. As a consequence, girls have less access to math and science experiences than do boys, because girls receive less constructive attention within math and science courses and ultimately choose fewer overall.

Given the practices of teachers and counselors, the gender mix of positions in schools, and a host of other factors, girls have neither adequate knowledge nor sufficient social support to enjoy genuine equality of educational opportunity. Thus the attempt to justify gender inequality as an outcome of choice, like the attempt to justify it as natural, also fails.

HUMANIST VERSUS GYNOCENTRIC FEMINISM

Gender inequality in education, then, is indeed an injustice that begs for a remedy, and it is logical to look in the direction of feminism to find one. Feminism, of course, comes in many varieties and is marked these days by significant internecine conflict. In education, however, two versions have been predominant in setting the terms of the debate: humanist (or liberal) and gynocentric (or relational).[2] In this section, I describe these versions of feminism, criticize them, and identify their central disagreement. This serves to lay the foundation for the subsequent section, in which I suggest that the disagreement might be resolved by appeal to the participatory educational ideal.

Humanist Feminism

According to Iris Marion Young (1990b, chap. 5), humanist feminism has been the dominant feminist perspective of the 19th and 20th centuries; it "defines women's oppression as the inhibition and distortion of women's potential by a society that allows the self-development of men" (p. 73). Appealing to celebrated feminist Simone de Beauvoir, Young characterizes this view as seeking to permit women to have the same opportunity as men to transcend, through free activity, the roles to which they are confined by cultural norms and expectations.

If this perspective is applied to education, females should have opportunities equal to those of males to pursue whatever educational avenues they choose. One interpretation is thus the formal interpretation of equality of educational opportunity that seeks to remove obstacles that prevent females from exercising free educational choices. This is the basic thrust of Title IX (Salamone, 1986) and is fairly representative of where gender equality in education now stands with respect to federal law (Stromquist, 1993). As we have already seen on several occasions, the formal interpretation is seriously flawed.

This leaves the compensatory interpretation under humanist feminism. This interpretation is sensitive to certain features of the context of choice and requires that these features be changed so as to provide girls and women with more meaningful kinds of educational opportunities. For example, the compensatory interpretation would embrace special scholarships, affirmative action to achieve better balance between teachers and administrators, greater teacher attention to girls in classrooms, and so forth. Relying on the assumptions that no natural gender differences exist and that unequal patterns are a reliable marker of unequal opportunities, its basic aim is to achieve equal gender patterns.

The problem with this interpretation is that it draws the wrong conclusion from libertarianism's shortcomings. Attempting merely to equalize existing patterns can exacerbate, because it can mask, fundamental sources of inequality that result from women's historical exclusion from participation in designing the basic institutions of society, including education. To reiterate Janet Radcliff Richards's (1980) observation: "If a group is kept out of doing something for long enough, it is overwhelmingly likely that activities . . . will develop in a way unsuited to the excluded group" (pp. 113–114). To now ignore the history through which institutions arose and "compensate" girls and women with special scholarships, affirmative action, and other special help programs so that they may fairly compete masks the kind of pervasive gender bias that underlies educational institutions.

Consider in this vein Jane Roland Martin's (1982) critique of the "ideal of the educated person," an ideal that she believes underpins the current educational system. Tracing the roots of this ideal to Plato, Martin contends that it incorporates the traditional masculine traits of rationality, autonomy, and self-control at the expense of the traditional feminine virtues of care and connection with others. Consequently, it values the "productive processes" of society over the "reproductive processes." Martin observes, furthermore, that shifting from the notion of the "educated man" to the notion of the "educated person" in the name of gender neutrality simply covers up the implicitly gendered nature of the ideal, making it more difficult to detect (see also Kymlicka, 1990; Noddings, 1990). Finally, she believes that providing females and males with an equal education in terms of such an ideal has at least two untoward consequences. First, it gives each a lopsided education in which preparation for the reproductive processes is missing. Second, insofar as traits are "genderized," girls and women who do manage to do well are denigrated for taking on the masculine traits the ideal incorporates.

To illustrate this more concretely, consider the admonition to educators to treat boys and girls equally and to provide girls with additional resources and help in math and science.[3] It may do little good to give girls extra resources and help if these are devoted to preparing them for a curriculum and modes of interaction that are foreign or hostile to who they are. What good does it do to ask girls more questions and to engage them more actively in classroom work if they find the classroom and the curriculum to be out of touch with their experiences and interests and to even devalue them? Even if the practices themselves are changed to include cooperative rather than competitive methods of teaching in order to, say, accommodate girls' "learning styles," this is not likely to achieve the desired results if the goals of education remain the same—goals rooted in competition and the traditional ideal of the educated person (Noddings, 1992; Shakeshaft, 1986).

The humanist model, then, remains committed to the status quo, even when it is associated with the compensatory interpretation of equality of educational opportunity (though less thoroughly so than when it is associated with the formal interpretation). Although motivated by the laudable aim of achieving equality, the humanist model fails to consider the historical antecedents of the present educational system and the practices and ideals it incorporates. As a consequence, the humanist model provides girls and women with educational opportunities that are either hollow (under the formal interpretation) or costly (under the compensatory interpretation).

Gynocentric Feminism

Gynocentric feminism is a variant of feminism that defines women's oppression as "the devaluation of women's experience by a masculine culture [and that] argues for the superiority of the values embodied in traditionally female experience" (Young, 1990b, chap. 5, pp. 73–74). According to Young, this perspective is much more recent than humanist feminism (beginning in the mid to late 1970s) and was significantly spurred by Carol Gilligan's (1982) critique of Kohlbergian moral psychology.[4]

Gilligan's (1982) basic thesis is that women have their own "voice," tied to their own kind of development, and it is different from, though not inferior to, men's voice. In general, women emphasize care and attention to particularity, with an eye toward preserving and fostering human relationships; men emphasize rights and universal principles, with an eye toward preserving autonomy and resolving conflicts fairly. Other empirical researchers have extended Gilligan's basic thesis beyond moral reasoning to encompass differences between girls and boys in learning and thinking patterns in general, concluding that females prefer "connected" to "separate" knowing across all contexts (Belenky et al., 1986).

This body of research is highly controversial, in terms of both its methodological and its philosophical assumptions (especially the extensions of Gilligan). Nonetheless, it has prompted much reflection about how schooling might afford girls greater equality, particularly in light of the numerous difficulties that attend various apologies for the status quo. No one has been more influential or had more things to say on this perspective as it applies to education than Nel Noddings.

In her 1984 book *Caring*, Noddings announces that she will reject an ethics of principle, the "approach of the detached one, of the father," the perspective that has historically dominated Western philosophy and law. In its place she develops an approach that establishes caring as the ethical ideal, the "approach of the mother." Unlike Gilligan's, Noddings's concerns are philosophical as opposed to psychological. Although she explicitly labels the ethics of care "feminine" and believes it much more typical of women than of men, she contends that Gilligan's empirical hypothesis need not be established in order for her philosophical thesis to be correct.

Noddings (1984) advances four general criticisms of an ethics of principle that recur in various ways and that complement one another throughout *Caring*. In addition to identifying what she rejects, these four criticisms also go a long way toward delineating her alternative view.

First, Noddings (1984) contends that an ethics of principle exhibits hierarchical reasoning such that ethical argumentation begins with isolated individuals and then proceeds ''as if it were governed by the logical necessity characteristic of geometry'' (p. 5). For Noddings, ethical reflection begins in a different place—with the ''natural caring'' that is fundamental to the ''human condition''—and cannot proceed by focusing on isolated individuals. Instead, individuals must be viewed as inherently existing in relationship to others, and ethical reflection must proceed in a way that pays close attention to this fact.

Second, an ethics of principle is abstract. Ethical principles are applied impartially, without regard to the contingencies that define morally problematic situations. According to an ethics of care, this severely distorts ethical deliberation, because individuals neither can nor should ignore the special attachments and obligations that grow out of their relationships to family, friends, community, and profession. For example, it would be somewhat odd, and by no means obviously praiseworthy, for the parents of a child with a disability to dispassionately agree with those who would deny that child special educational services on the grounds that this is the conclusion an impartial application of principle yields.

Third, an ethics of principle requires universalizability. That is, once endorsed, ethical principles must be applicable to all ''relevantly similar'' cases. But because principles are by their very nature ambiguous, universalizability encourages ignoring the peculiarities of given situations by forcing them to fit this or that ethical principle and forcing them to be ''similar'' when actually they are unique. In this way, an ethics of principle is legalistic, backward looking, and blind to the kind of creativity and sensitivity required to deal with new situations for which the principles derived from past deliberations are inadequate. This does not imply that an ethics of care dismisses ethical principles altogether—rules against lying, cheating, stealing, and so forth—but that it is quick to abandon principles when they give no guidance or when they conflict with the ideal of caring. For thinkers such as Noddings, caring is the ethical universal.

Finally, from the perspective of an ethics of care, an ethics of principle serves to inhibit rather than to foster caring relationships, for devotion to principles can lead to separateness and to placing principles above persons. As Noddings (1984) asserts:

> Wherever there is a principle, there is implied its exception and, too often, principles function to separate us from each other. We may become dangerously self-righteous when we perceive ourselves as holding a precious principle not held by the other. The other may then be devalued and treated "differently." Our ethic of caring will not permit this to happen. (p. 5)

In an ethics of care, one starts with concrete relationships and individuals; then one works outward to whatever principles might be reasonable. Noddings (1984) illustrates this point in dramatic fashion when she recounts the story of Manlius.

> . . . Manlius [was] a Roman commander who laid down harsh rules for the conduct of his legions. One of the first to disobey a rule about leaving camp to engage in individual combat was his own son. In compliance with the rules, Manlius ordered the execution of his son. A principle had been violated; for this violation, X must be executed. That "X" was replaced by "my son" gave Manlius no release from obedience to the principle. Why, then, did he not think concretely before establishing the rule? Why do men so often lay out their own clear paths to tragedy? The one-caring would want to think carefully about the establishment of rules and even more carefully about the prescription of penalties. Indeed, she would prefer to establish a climate of cooperative "we-ness" so that rules and penalties might be kept to a minimum. For her, the hypothetical is filled in with real persons, and, thus, her rules are tempered a priori with thoughts of those in her inner circle. (p. 44)

In addition to being the starting point, concrete relationships and individuals are also the ending point, meaning that principles are always subject to being superseded by the demands of caring. Noddings (1984) continues the story of Manlius as follows:

> A stranger might, then, be spared death because she [the one-caring] would not visit death upon her own child. She does not, in whatever personal agony, inflict death upon her child in devotion to either principle or abstract entity. (p. 44)

In her subsequent book, the *Challenge to Care in Schools*, Noddings (1992) brings the ethical framework of *Caring* to bear on the current nature of public schooling in the United States. She is critical of, among other things, the emphasis on competition and testing; the disciplinary knowledge that defines a liberal education; the same education for all in the name of equality of educational opportunity; and the evaluation of virtually every activity (even providing hungry children with food) in terms of how well it contributes to mastering the prescribed curriculum—characteristics that are presumably definitive of a male-oriented ethics of principles. In place of this model of schooling, Noddings suggests that we take seriously the demands of an ethics of care and that we think of educating public school students on the model of educating the members of a large heterogeneous family, the paradigmatic case of an institution defined in terms of relationships rather than principles. Denouncing "shallow" educational responses to "deep social change," she proposes that we radically reorganize the curriculum, the modes of instruction, and the structural features of schooling.

Noddings (1992) notes that the emphasis today on the academic disciplines benefits the college-bound at the expense of the majority who will not attend college. She proposes reorganizing the curriculum around what she calls "centers of care," with the aim of creating "competent, caring, loving, and lovable people" (p. xvi). Such centers include caring for the self; caring for the inner circle; caring for strangers and distant others; caring for animals, plants, and the earth; caring for the human-made world; and caring for ideas. Noddings believes that cognitive activity should be a large part of what schooling is about, but, consistent with the arguments of *Caring*, she stipulates affective attachment as the focal point from which cognitive reflection must begin.

Instruction should be reoriented so as to emphasize four components: modeling, dialogue, practice, and confirmation. Noddings (1992) observes that teachers unavoidably serve as role models in their teaching as well as in general dealings with others. She notes that this is an especially important part of schooling organized around caring because so much depends on fostering human relationships. Although she concedes that didactic instruction can have its place, she is generally dismissive of what Paulo Freire (1983) so aptly calls "banking education." She contends that students must be immersed in genuine dialogue that is truly open-ended and responsive to their interests and experiences. Becoming accomplished at this kind of dialogue requires adopting the right attitudes and "mentalities," which, in turn, requires practice—by the nature of this kind of dialogue, students cannot be told the "right answers" or how to deduce them. Finally, appealing to Martin Buber, she contends that teachers must confirm the best that they find in their students. Measuring them all by the same yardstick and focusing on their failings are anathema to Noddings.

The structure of schools should be reorganized so as to engender much greater continuity, specifically, continuity of purpose, curriculum, place, and people. The kind of curriculum and instruction envisaged by Noddings (1992) requires attention to how attitudes and knowledge are connected and build upon each other over time. This explains the need for continuity of purpose and curriculum. The kind of curriculum and instruction that Noddings envisages also requires close and trusting relationships that take time to forge. This explains the need for continuity of place and people.

Noddings (1992) suggests that simply rearranging things so that students would remain in a given school and with the same teachers long enough to gain a sense of belonging would go a long way toward achieving continuity of place and people. Achieving continuity of purpose and curriculum would require more substantive changes in present educational practices and accepted beliefs about the nature and aims of education, the most important being a shift away from the emphasis on achievement and the academic disciplines toward an emphasis on caring and centers of care.

Given the fundamental changes Noddings calls for, her proposal for remaking schooling could hardly be confused with a compensatory interpretation of equality, much less a formal interpretation.[5] Instead, she would achieve gender equality indirectly, by infusing the feminine perspective throughout the curriculum, instruction, and structure of schools. In this connection, it should be observed that Noddings's proposal is not focused exclusively on gender equality. Remaking schooling in the way she proposes promotes a morally better situation in general. Not only girls but also boys and minorities should benefit.

Noddings's (1992) proposal has much to recommend it. It is powerful, potentially fruitful, and, if implemented, would surely be a significant advance over the way schooling is presently conducted. Nonetheless, it presents two significant difficulties. The first is her considerably less than convincing critique of an ethics of principles. Although an ethics of care is legitimate and may indeed conflict with the demands of an ethics of principles, it does not follow that the latter should be abandoned (Benhabib, 1992; Hampshire, 1983; Kymlicka, 1990, chap. 7; Larmore, 1987; Nagel, 1986, 1991).

Recall the story of Manlius. This example is specifically designed by Noddings (1984) to call into question ethical principles, equality and impartiality in particular, that require treating everyone the same regardless of the concrete personal relationships that exist. Thus it is not simply Manlius's rules that are at issue here (which, no doubt, can be criticized as generally too harsh) but that he was not swayed by having them indifferently applied to his own son.

Manlius is indeed open to moral criticism, but it should be noted that much of the sting would be taken out of the example if Manlius had withdrawn himself from the decision regarding the punishment of his son, particularly if he had gone on to advocate leniency. The general point here is that the degree to which it is morally appropriate (as well as psychologically possible) for a person to assume an impartial perspective depends on the position that the person occupies within existing relationships. That it is sometimes morally inappropriate to adopt an impartial perspective does not mean that it always is. (Compare the perspective a Supreme Court Justice should adopt when she acts as a mother with that she should assume when she acts as a jurist.)

Consider the consequences of completely jettisoning the demands of impartiality in favor of the demands of concrete community and personal relationships. The result can be only a blinkered moral perspective. Because it is very difficult to make sense of moral obligations to strangers without appeal to some measure of impartial concern, strangers outside the orbit of established relationships are effectively excluded from consideration.

It is noteworthy that similar reservations about Noddings's views on caring originate from within the feminist project itself. For example, Carol Gilligan (1982) denies the putative incompatibility between an ethics of care and an ethics of principles with respect to moral psychology (see also Flanagan & Jackson, 1990). Susan Moller Okin (1989), a liberal feminist philosopher, defends the view that an ethics of principles can (must) be built upon a foundation of caring. Taking a different tack, Iris Marion Young (1990b, chap. 5) contends that, however unintentionally, gynocentric feminism may actually serve more to rationalize and perpetuate women's oppression than to eliminate it.[6]

In *Challenge*, Noddings's (1992) view appears to be considerably less gynocentric than in *Caring* (1984). For example, she stresses the need for open-ended dialogue that incorporates the diversity of interests and perspectives (see also Noddings, 1990). She also takes seriously enough the problem of obligations to distant others to propose it as one of her curricular "centers of care." Nonetheless, there is substantial continuity between *Caring* and *Challenge*: Noddings's mistrust of an ethics of principles remains strong, and it is implicated in the sharp distinction she makes between "educational" and "political" rationales. This distinction is, in turn, implicated in the second significant difficulty with Noddings's view: It glosses over the fundamental problem of the political function of schooling in a democratic society.

Although Noddings gestures in the direction of a political function for schooling—she endorses the importance of fostering "civil responsibility," for example—most of what she has to say directly on the issue is markedly critical and dismissive. She focuses her criticisms on two viewpoints: those exemplified in the *Paideia Proposal* (Adler et al., 1982) and in certain neo-Marxist scholarship.

In the *Paideia Proposal*, Mortimer Adler and his associates (1982) maintain that traditional liberal education is a requirement for citizens to function effectively in a democratic society and that therefore a liberal arts curriculum ought to be provided to all. Noddings (1992) rejects both of these claims. She rejects the notion that being an effective citizen depends on mastering the traditional liberal arts curriculum on the grounds that the connection between the two is quite tenuous. Mathematics, for example, is central to the liberal education curriculum but is not required of effective citizenship (at least beyond basic calculation skills): "Lots of very nice people, even very good citizens," she writes, "find mathematics difficult and unpleasant" (p. 29). And she rejects the notion that a liberal education should be provided to everyone (indeed, she questions whether it should be provided to anyone) on the grounds that individuals have different interests and talents and that those who are not suited for liberal education are inevitably going to fare poorly when they are required to undergo it.

Neo-Marxists, according to Noddings (1992), defend providing all students with a liberal education on the grounds that it encompasses the kind of knowledge associated with power and privilege. Accordingly, not providing it is unjust. She responds by claiming that we ought to distinguish "educational" from "political" rationales for educational programs and that we should be guided primarily by the former. Political rationales should not be used to foist a liberal arts curriculum on children for whom it is ill-suited and for whom failure is bound to be the result. She also observes that the knowledge associated with power and privilege can and does change, and is most likely to do so in ways that keep it in the same hands.

Noddings's (1992) criticisms of the program of the *Paideia Proposal* (1982) and of the neo-Marxist position (at least the kind she singles out) both hit the mark. However, her sweeping distinction between "educational" and "political" rationales for educational programs unduly limits her treatment of the available alternatives. And the manner in which she seems to depoliticize schooling and render it immune from political criticism is truly worrisome. Surely it is an educational *and* a political concern if schooling serves to reproduce existing forms of injustice and domination.

The flaw in Noddings's argument—the flaw that, interestingly, gives it plausibility—is her implicit identification of "political" rationales for given forms of educational systems with what Young (1990a) calls the "distributive paradigm" of justice, a paradigm that undergirds various liberal conceptions of justice. The problem with this paradigm is that it ignores the processes by which distributions of society's goods come to exist and focuses instead on equalizing unequal distributions that result from such processes. As Noddings (1992) rightly observes in this connection (and reminiscent of the previous criticisms of the compensatory interpretation of equality of educational opportunity), political rationales for education should avoid "the folly of trying to redistribute either monetary or cultural wealth without addressing the basically evil value structure that undergirds structures of domination" (p. 33).

But the problem is not with political rationales per se; it is with the particular kinds that Noddings (1992) singles out and with the resulting forced choice that is encouraged between humanist feminism (and equality) and gynocentric feminism (and caring). Noddings herself suggests that feminism has entered a "transformational" phase characterized by the desire to move beyond this forced choice.[7] Such a transformational strategy may be applied straightforwardly to the problem of the "political" versus "educational" aims of schooling. The key, of course, is construing political aims in a way that avoids the kinds of criticisms Noddings advances. This is precisely what the participatory educational ideal can do.

TRANSFORMATION AND THE PARTICIPATORY EDUCATIONAL IDEAL

In her 1993 presidential address to the Philosophy of Education Society, Noddings (1993b) echoed themes from both *Caring* (1984) and *Challenge* (1992), but she also took on the question of educational equality more directly, arguing, in particular, that excellence ought to supplant equality as the guiding educational ideal.

The crux of Noddings's (1993b) argument is her identification of *equality* with *sameness*, in terms of both the curriculum and the goals held for different students. As she observes in her critique of the *Paideia Proposal* (1982), pursuing this kind of equality guarantees that many students will fail. Alternatively, borrowing from Thomas Green, Noddings maintains we could make students equal by providing them equally miserable conditions.[8] Noddings identifies *excellence*, by contrast, with varying the curriculum and its goals so as to coincide with the different things different students might be good at and might want to pursue.

Perhaps the identification of equality with sameness infects the general public discourse about education, but this identification is most unlikely among philosophers of education, who take quite the opposite view. (And consider how "excellence" functions in the public discourse, an issue I return to in the Conclusion.) Dewey (1981a), for example (whom, interestingly, Noddings often cites approvingly), urges that equality not be confused with "that kind of mathematical or physical equivalence in virtue of which any one element may be substituted for another" (p. 625). The point, again, is that equality must be "worth wanting," and Noddings's variety most assuredly is not (at least not by any but the privileged).

Given the way she sets this up, it is no wonder that Noddings (1993b) would want to abandon equality as the guide to the "educational conversation." The problem is that her characterization of what "advocates of equality" mean by equality, and what they want in its name, is more than a little questionable. The influential theory of educational equality Amy Gutmann (1987) develops in *Democratic Education* provides a case in point.

My embrace and characterization of an educational threshold in the last chapter owe much to Gutmann. Here I will reiterate certain aspects of the threshold and expand others with an eye toward responding to Noddings's (1993b) critique of equality. Chief among my aims is to show how a conception of education grounded in equality need not result in entrenching the status quo ante nor in excluding the voices and interests of girls, women, and others. On the contrary, it can and should serve to foster a transformation of present arrangements.

One of the features of a threshold of educational equality is that it limits in two ways the degree to which sameness should be the goal: Sameness is but one among many educational goals, "democratic character," in Gutmann's case (1987), and it is desirable to only a threshold level. It should be noted that Noddings herself believes that *some* educational aims should be common—literacy, basic skills in mathematics, for instance—in addition to the capacity and disposition to care.

Furthermore, as I argued in the previous section, Noddings's view of the political aims of education is unduly narrow. When we examine what goes into Gutmann's "core political purpose" of fostering democratic character, we find much with which Noddings would agree. For example, both endorse greater participation by all concerned in negotiating and enacting the curriculum, a pedagogy steeped in critical dialogue, and the fostering of dispositions toward tolerance, nonrepression, nondiscrimination, and nonviolence.

Gutmann's (1987) analysis of "sexist" education provides a more specific illustration of how a participatory (transformational) view can accommodate Noddings's concerns. Gutmann defines sexist educational practices as "those that serve . . . to restrict the quality or quantity of democratic education received by girls (or women) relative to that received by boys (or men)" (p. 111). So long as we stick to the *quantity* of education, Gutmann may be seen to be identifying equality with sameness. There is a sense of the *quality* of education in which this is true as well—for instance, how accomplished teachers are. But there is another sense of quality that goes much deeper than this. As Gutmann remarks in connection with the gender distribution of teachers and administrators in the public schools,

> [A]s long as women are hired as elementary-school teachers in far greater proportions than men, and men are hired as school administrators in far greater proportions than women, schools will teach children that "men rule women and women rule children." . . . Girls learn that it is normal for them to rule children, but abnormal for them to rule men. Boys learn the opposite lesson. The democratic problem lies not in the content of the lesson per se, but in its repressive nature: the lessons reinforce uncritical acceptance of an established set of sex stereotypes and unreflective rejection of reasonable (and otherwise available) alternatives. (pp. 113–114)

Remedying *this* problem requires going well beyond equality as sameness.Because repression is not confined to overt silencing but may also be found in institutional arrangement as well as in the hidden curriculum, schools require broad—and deep—change of a kind that disrupts and transforms traditional gender assumptions and relationships in schools.[9]

In relation to this, Gutmann, too, has been influenced by insights of gynocentric feminism. Although Gutmann is no doubt less suspicious than Noddings of a "morality of principles"[10]—the putatively male-oriented morality that elevates impartiality and commitment to abstract principle to the highest place—she has her reservations, particularly in the context of schooling. She thus agrees with Noddings that schools should not base moral and political education on such a conception of morality. She doubts the ability of schools to teach a morality of principles successfully, and she criticizes the pedagogical approaches associated with such teaching for neglecting the development of moral character. Moreover, she denies that the morality of principle is morality in its highest form and that it is required to promote democracy.

In place of a morality of principles, Gutmann (1987) advocates a "morality of association"[11] as the moral-political aim to which schools should aspire. This conception is marked by the virtues of "empathy, trust, fairness, and benevolence," virtues, she emphasizes, that are "at least as common in women as men" (p. 62). It shares much with Noddings's morality of caring.

Noddings (1992, 1993b), then, significantly overstates the tensions between equality and political aims, on the one hand, and caring and educational aims, on the other—tensions that are closely paralleled in the alternatives of humanistic and gynocentric feminisms. If I am right, "political" and "educational" justifications for the conduct of schooling are not mutually exclusive. On the contrary, the two are thoroughly intertwined. The needed transformation of gender arrangements Noddings (1990) endorses can be effected only by a strategy that renders participation meaningful—by a strategy, in other words, that renders educational opportunities equally worth wanting.

CONCLUSION

This chapter examined gender equality (the lack thereof) in the schools as an important issue in its own right. The analysis was limited, to be sure. For one thing, not all girls and women recognize the existence of a problem to be fixed. For another, those who do are by no means univocal on what the problem is or what shape the remedy should take, often because they differ on how to understand and rank gender with respect to other sources of oppression. Much more needs to be said about these and other issues relating to gender and education, but I must leave that to others more inclined and better equipped to take on the many dimensions of this immense and complex topic.

This chapter also had the general purpose of refining the participatory educational ideal. I advanced the view that the participatory interpretation of equality of educational opportunity—which emphasizes the political dimensions of education—can accommodate and be enriched by a view like that of Noddings, which emphasizes the personal dimensions. This helps reconcile what is sometimes viewed as an unbridgeable divide between liberalism and feminism, and helps render more concrete what is required to include historically silenced voices in deciding what are to count as educational opportunities worth wanting.

In Chapter 4, I take up other sources of inequality, such as race, ethnicity, language, sexual orientation, and religious belief, and grapple with the constellation of issues that fall under the general rubric of multicultural education. Paralleling the strategy I used in this chapter, I examine multicultural education as an important issue in its own right but also employ the analysis to further explicate the participatory educational ideal.

CHAPTER 4

Multiculturalism

Pocho . . . *they called me. Sometimes playfully, teasingly, under the tender diminutive—mi* pochito. *Sometimes not so playfully, mockingly,* Pocho. *(A Spanish dictionary defines that word as an adjective meaning "colorless" or "bland." But I heard it as a noun, naming the Mexican-American who, in becoming an American, forgot his native society.) "!Pocho!" the lady in the Mexican food store muttered, shaking her head.*
—Richard Rodriguez, Hunger of Memory

I think white people think education is good, but Indian people often have a different view . . . they see it as something that draws students away from who they are. . . .

I would like to tell them that education shouldn't try and make me into something I'm not.
—Delbert Thunderwolf, Interview with William G. Tierney,
"The College Experience of Native Americans"

At Groton [school], I'm Puerto Rican—and that's not good. At home, I'm white—and that's not good. So, what is good?
—Jo Vega, Videotaped interview, American Dream at Groton

These remarks by a Mexican American writer, a Native American community college student, and a Puerto Rican high school student, respectively, drive home the point that the opportunities educational institutions offer are not equally worth wanting solely because they are there for the taking. Depending on the context of choice in which given opportunities exist, exercising them can exact markedly higher "opportunity costs" for certain individuals than for others. For they can come at the expense of one's personal identity and continued participation in one's cultural group.

There are three responses to this problem. The first is to discount the opportunity costs incurred by certain groups and to endeavor to bring them into the "melting pot" of American (U.S.) culture. This culture is to be embodied in and promoted through universal educational ideals in the public schools. This approach can, and often does, include good-faith attempts to mitigate the perceived disadvantages that certain groups experience.

The second response is to react against the first by abandoning the idea that there can be any universal educational ideals—any educational opportunities equally worth wanting—that can be legitimately promoted by the public schools. In this view, such ideals inherently buttress hegemony and oppression.

The third response is to steer a middle course between the first two. In this view, universal educational ideals for public schools are both defensible and required but must differ in content and justification from those associated with the customary melting pot idea. This is the view I advance in this chapter.

THE MELTING POT

Tracing its roots to the beginnings of the United States, Arthur Schlesinger (1992) contends the melting pot or "one people" interpretation has "thus far managed to keep American society whole" (p. 16). But this idea, he contends, is now being challenged by the "ethnic interpretation" (also abusively referred to as the "cult of ethnicity"). As a consequence of its putative embrace of separatism, this view poses a serious threat to U.S. society in general and public schools in particular. Schlesinger warns,

> The militants of ethnicity now contend that a main objective of public education should be the protection, strengthening, celebration, and perpetuation of ethnic origins and identities. Separatism, however, nourishes prejudices, magnifies differences and stirs antagonisms. The consequent increase in ethnic and racial conflict lies behind the hullabaloo over "multiculturalism" and "political correctness" . . .
>
> One wonders: Will the center hold? or will the melting pot give way to the Tower of Babel? (pp. 17–18)

Schlesinger's general themes are widely embraced. The idea of assimilating all children into the intellectual disciplines in order to forge a cohesive democratic citizenry is a major theme of Mortimer Adler and associates' (1982) well-known *Paideia Proposal*. This idea (though with a much more marked economic emphasis) has been echoed since *A Nation at Risk* (1983) in the government proposals that emphasize more rigorous and uniform curricula, standards, and assessments grounded in the traditional disciplines. In a different vein, Diane Ravitch (1990) has joined Schlesinger in criticizing multiculturalists for abandoning the principle of *e pluribus unum* in favor of the principle of *e pluribus plures*, and for abusing and distorting history in the name of building self-esteem. E. D. Hirsch (1988), however, provides the best comprehensive statement of this stance toward multicultural education. In his acclaimed *Cultural Literacy*, he develops in one sustained argument the various themes spread across other "conservative" thinkers.[1]

Like Schlesinger (1992), Hirsch (1988) warns that multicultural education is inherently fragmentary and issues similar warnings about the coming Tower of Babel. His general thesis is that schools should foster a uniform cultural literacy to avert this. And this is not only a good for the nation, not only a collective good. It is also a good for individuals, especially the disadvantaged who, because they are denied "cultural literacy," are denied equality of opportunity.

An Individual Good?

Hirsch's (1988) view exemplifies a paradigmatic case of the compensatory interpretation of equality of educational opportunity. That is, there is an educational good—cultural literacy—in terms of which certain groups are put at a disadvantage by virtue of things such as their cultural, linguistic, or economic status. The solution is to provide needed assistance in order to mitigate the effects of such disadvantages (Hirsch endorses Head Start, for example, and in general believes early education is essential).

In the previous two chapters I criticized the compensatory interpretation of equality of educational opportunity both in general and with respect to its specific application to gender. The basic criticism is that however well-intentioned and justified in certain situations, the compensatory interpretation too often entails disproportionate opportunity costs for those who are the target of compensation. And it is also ineffective. These criticisms apply straightforwardly to Hirsch's stance regarding multicultural education.

Although Hirsch (1988) nowhere addresses these criticisms directly, he does advance an argument that, if sound, would serve to diminish their force significantly. The argument is that, on balance, assimilation is the best alternative even from the perspective of individuals who must pay the extra price. The argument has two basic threads. Hirsch first criticizes the idea that skills ought to be emphasized over content (an idea that he attributes largely to Dewey). He then buttresses this with his interpretation of what the recent findings of cognitive psychology, particularly schema theory, reveal.

Underlying Hirsch's (1988) argument is the general premise that public education ought to be guided by a uniform ideal that, if realized, would produce a cohesive democratic society in which all could participate and whose goods all could enjoy. According to him, such an ideal must include a considerable amount of content—names, dates, places, maxims, aphorisms—as distinct from reasoning skills alone (contra the way Dewey would putatively have it). Indeed, Hirsch believes that children actually enjoy "piling up information" (again, contra Dewey). But even if they didn't, he contends, educators would have a duty to supply them with what they so sorely need for their well-being. And this is where schema theory comes into play. Individuals are able to comprehend and communicate only against a background of shared knowledge. Certain (Deweyian) intuitions notwithstanding, this is true even in the case of what otherwise appear to be discrete, unrelated bits of knowledge.

Not to put too fine a point on it, Hirsch gets Dewey flat wrong. (Admittedly, some—many—educators interpret Dewey in precisely the way Hirsch does, but this is no excuse for him.) In *Experience and Education*, written late in his career and in response to just the kind of misinterpretation exemplified by Hirsch, Dewey (1938) makes crystal clear that he does not endorse a skills approach as an exclusive alternative to a content approach. On the contrary, he chides this as "either-or" thinking and explicitly rejects it in favor of an educational theory that, in Hirsch's terms, balances skills and content.

More is at issue here than just setting the record straight. Many educational theorists, myself included, find much that is relevant to the current scene in Dewey's political and educational theories. Properly interpreted, Dewey's views pose a significant challenge to Hirsch's.

Dewey (1938) identifies two basic principles of experience: "continuity" and "interaction." The former depicts all experiences as continuous with and shaped by experiences that have come before; the latter depicts each experience as determined by the interaction between an individual's state and the conditions in the environment that prompt it. Although Dewey takes these to be ubiquitous features of experience, his primary focus is on how to manipulate conditions in schools so that the experiences to be had are "educative." Briefly, providing such experiences requires having some goals for students in view (Dewey emphasizes problem solving, or "growth," but also includes content knowledge), while taking into account the need to pay attention to what individuals bring to their encounter with schools and to tailoring the content and form of instruction accordingly.

Although they express it in different terms, Dewey and Hirsch are in general agreement regarding the importance of background knowledge. Why, then, is Hirsch so critical of Dewey? And why would Dewey reject Hirsch's proposal (as I think he most certainly would)?

Aside from my claim that Hirsch (1988) simply misrepresents Dewey (1938), there is an additional reason for disagreement. Hirsch employs schema theory like a hired cab, which he discharges when he reaches his desired destination—the schoolhouse door. Children begin school, after all, not as blank slates, waiting for schools to write whatever they choose, but with schema—linguistic and cultural, to name two of the more important ones—already in place. Moreover, because children spend a good deal of their time outside schools, in their communities and families, such schema are likely to be reinforced. Hirsch provides absolutely no reason for ignoring these facts, for why, in terms of his own appeal to schema theory, the advice to inculcate cultural literacy shouldn't be rejected as grounded in faulty psychology. By contrast, Dewey clearly recognizes these facts and incorporates them into his view. Thus he sees "a single course of studies for all progressive schools" as "out of the question," for "it would mean abandoning the fundamental principle of connection with life experiences" (p. 78).

Hirsch's (1988) recommendation, then, looks a lot like the "traditional" view that Dewey (1938) criticizes: Educators determine what is worth knowing and, with no consideration of the makeup of the learners they are teaching, set about to inculcate it. Hirsch differs from many traditionalists, however, in how he determines what is worth knowing. In particular, his criterion is not a "prescriptive" one—what qualifies as exemplary thought throughout the ages, for instance—but a "descriptive" one—what literate Americans in fact know. His argument for inculcating cultural literacy, then, is largely utilitarian. From the point of view of disadvantaged individuals, it is not as if their culture or language is inferior in some fundamental sense; it is just in their best interest to master the knowledge associated with power and success in U.S. society as it presently exists.

Although this is a good piece of advice for the disadvantaged,[2] it is far from an adequate defense of Hirsch's (1988) general position. First, he would have to move much closer to Dewey (1938) regarding how to inculcate cultural literacy effectively; he would have to be more faithful to his own claims about the importance of background knowledge to learning. Second, the advice is wholly contingent on the way things are.

(In this vein, it parallels advising a woman trying to advance in her career never to wear her emotions on her sleeve and to avoid being labeled a feminist.) Even if Hirsch's version of cultural literacy starts off being wholly "descriptive," a dubious proposition, it ends up as the justification for his clearly "prescriptive" claims about the direction public education should take. Hirsch again gets where he wants to go and then discharges the cab. In this case, however, he then hires another one.

Hirsch's (1988) idea that there is nothing fundamental about the contents of cultural literacy, that it is just a fact to be dealt with, is naive and insensitive (and, it would seem, all too convenient for someone positioned as he is). There is a significant tension between this "When in Rome *be* a Roman" strategy and the warnings he issues regarding the discord and fragmentation that would attend a failure to inculcate a uniform cultural literacy. For such a threat would be nonexistent if people could be as prudential and calculating regarding how to define themselves as Hirsch thinks they can and should be.

A Collective Good?

Although Hirsch (1988) denies that he is "directly concerned with the question of bilingualism" (p. 93), language looms large in his argument. It is part of the shared cultural literacy, without which nations are marked by fragmentation and strife. As he puts it,

> In America the reality is that we have not yet properly achieved *mono*literacy, much less multiliteracy. Because of the demands created by technology we need effective monoliteracy more than ever. Linguistic pluralism would make sense for us only on the questionable assumption that our civil peace and national effectiveness could survive multilingualism. But in fact, multilingualism enormously increases cultural fragmentation, civil antagonism, illiteracy, and economic-technological ineffectiveness. . . .
>
> [W]ell-meaning bilingualism could unwittingly erect serious barriers to cultural literacy among our young people and therefore create serious barriers to universal literacy at a mature level. . . . In the best of all worlds, all Americans would be multiliterate. But surely the first step in that direction must be for all of us to become literate in our own national language and culture. (pp. 92–93)

Here, Hirsch's argument tilts away from the individual's good and toward the collective good—the good of the nation—and takes on a marked economic emphasis.

Now it is difficult to see what familiarity with the Mona Lisa (part of Hirsch's 1993 recommended first-grade curriculum) has to do with "technological-economic" effectiveness. Moreover, Hirsch (1988) blatantly begs the question with his reference to "our own language and culture." In my view, these objections are telling. I note them only in passing, however, for I want to focus on a different matter: Hirsch's characterization of the threat that multiculturalism/lingualism poses and his contention that inculcating cultural literacy is the best way to eliminate it.

Hirsch (1988) and like-minded thinkers give an account of history in which multiculturalism and multilingualism can serve only to tear nations apart. They tend to leave out of their account the very different historical conditions from which they wish to generalize. For example, Spanish is now the largest minority language in the United States. However, in contrast to the Quebecois of Canada and the Flemish of Belgium (two examples employed by Hirsch to illustrate the dangers of multilingualism), Spanish speakers do not comprise a uniform cultural group and they anglicize at a high rate (Baron, 1990). Hirsch and like-minded thinkers also tend to leave out of their account that efforts to promote monolingualism have typically employed coercive methods and have usually backfired. The former Soviet Union, with its official language policy, provides a good example here.

"Generally speaking," says Dennis Baron (1990), "linguistic friction and violence occur around the globe not where language rights are protected, but where they have been suppressed" (p. 180). This observation can easily be extended beyond language to include culture more generally, and it calls into question the dilemma that thinkers such as Hirsch pose: Either inculcate a shared language and culture or disintegrate as a nation. Indeed, it may well be more effective in the name of national survival to accommodate linguistic and cultural differences than to attempt to eliminate them. But even if accommodating such differences did come at some cost to national unity, this would not be sufficient to resolve the issue in Hirsch's favor. The range of outcomes associated with a policy of monoculturalism versus one of multiculturalism is unpredictable enough to make the deciding factor the injustice of requiring certain groups to absorb a disproportionate share of the costs.

THE ABANDONMENT OF UNIVERSAL EDUCATIONAL IDEALS

As I suggest in the introduction to this chapter, one response to the inadequacies of the melting pot idea is to abandon wholesale the search for universal educational ideals. Libertarianism provides one kind of justification for this view. I have already proffered a general critique of libertarianism and return to its shortcomings in subsequent chapters, particularly Chapter 7. Here I focus my attention on a second kind of justification for abandoning the search for universal educational ideals: the kind postmodernism provides.

To complicate matters, precisely who counts as a "postmodernist" thinker is by no means clear. Derrida, Foucault, and Lyotard seem to be on everyone's list; Rorty and Wittgenstein are clear cases for some (e.g., Beck, 1994); and others would even include Dewey (e.g., Doll, 1993). Trying to sort this out is not likely to bear fruit for present purposes, particularly insofar as the "postmodern condition" cuts across all facets of contemporary life. Thus I focus on two postmodernist themes that are especially germane here: incredulity toward metanarratives and decentering the self.

Incredulity Toward Metanarratives

In an unusual move for a postmodernist, Lyotard (1987) actually proffers a definition: "I define *postmodern* as incredulity toward metanarratives" (p. 74). Briefly, a metanarrative is a grand legitimating story, one important feature of which is its abstraction from time, place, and culture. Metanarratives include grand epistemological stories such as the inevitable progress of positivist science. They also include grand political stories, my concern here.

The Marxist and liberal traditions both count as metanarratives. Both embrace the goal of the emancipation of humankind and are regarded as highly suspect by postmodernists for precisely this reason. Because the goal of emancipation incorporates a peculiarly Western story, pursuing it serves, as Lyotard (1987) says, to "terrorize" people who had no part in writing it. It is, after all, a time-, place-, and culture-bound story of human existence and, accordingly, a very bad fit for those outside the confines it presumes. Worse, because modernity has spent itself, it is a bad story for Western societies themselves.

Michel Foucault (1987) shares Lyotard's (1987) attitude toward metanarratives and would supplant them with what he calls "geneology." Foucault's (1987) method is to unearth (he has also used the metaphor of archeology) the historical antecedents of the rationalization of modern institutions. For Foucault, rationality is irremediably historical and contingent, and there can be no extrahistorical touchstones—metanarratives—of the kind philosophers have sought since Plato. Similarly, no clear distinction (if any) can be made between knowledge and power. "Regimes of truth" inherently incorporate networks of power that facilitate "normalization," that is, "the production of docile and useful bodies to staff our offices, factories, schools and armies" (Baynes, Bohman, & McCarthy, 1987, p. 96).

However cursory this description of the postmodernist incredulity toward metanarratives, it is sufficient to explain the general criticism that so pervasively leaps to the minds of critics: that postmodernism is hopelessly nihilistic and cannot, if consistently held, justify any political projects whatsoever. For if all moral-political claims are thoroughly context-bound and simply masks for interests and power, are not any political projects postmodernists may advocate themselves possessed of these features? And is this general postmodernist perspective not a kind of metanarrative itself—a timeless story of the human condition?

I *do not mean* to suggest that postmodernists happily embrace moral-political silence. Foucault (1987) seeks through his form of analysis to displace seeming self-evidentness about normalcy and the practices that go with it, and he has a clear, albeit open-ended, political purpose here. For his part, Lyotard (1987) embraces the concept of justice but would replace the modernist interpretation, which consists in forging consensus ("homology"), with a postmodernist interpretation, which consists in facilitating the expression of difference ("parology"). I *do mean* to suggest that postmodernist responses such as these are inadequate. Quite simply, once the status quo has been dislocated and different voices have been heard, the question remains as to which of the alternatives that are opened up ought to be pursued.

If this is a serious problem for the moral-political project of postmodernists in general (and I think it is), it is even more so for postmodern educationists. As Burbules (1996) observes, education is inherently about growth and development and is therefore inherently goal-directed. Thus, however cautious educators can and ought to be about the norms, dispositions, attitudes, and knowledge they foster, foster some they must.

Perhaps recognition of Burbules's (1996) point explains why postmodernists in education are, by comparison to postmodernists more generally, relatively unabashed about embracing the project of ending oppression, and why they are less likely to limit themselves to deconstruction (but see Usher & Edwards, 1994). Unfortunately for them, this just brings the problem of nihilism into sharper relief. Postmodernist educationists face the dilemma of either having no grounds for opposing oppressive educational practices (wouldn't any opposition just be an expression of their own will to power?) or embracing *some* kind of overarching principle(s) upon which to base their opposition (against their avowals to the contrary).

Consider the following remark by Elisabeth Ellsworth (1992):

> [I]n a classroom in which "empowerment" is made dependent on rationalism, those perspectives that would question the political interests (sexism, racism, colonialism, for example) expressed and guaranteed by rationalism would be rejected as "irrational" (biased, partial). (p. 98)

People who criticize sexism, racism, and colonialism are uniformly dismissed as irrational by those whose goal is empowerment? Not in my experience. And what is the alternative to "rationalism"? As Benjamin Barber (1992) asks,

> How can . . . reformers think they will empower the voiceless by proving that voice is always a function of power? . . . How do they think the struggle for equality and justice can be waged with an epistemology that denies standing to reasons and normative rational terms . . . ? (p. 123)

In my view, there is no way for those who would reject rationalism across the board to respond adequately to Barber's questions, no way for them to avoid being condemned to moral-political silence. And this follows whether or not we supplant well-worn concepts like justice and rationality with voguish terms like standpoints and narratives. In the end, some overarching (and presumably rational) standpoint (conception of justice) must be embraced. And Ellsworth (1992) does exactly this when she proffers the following question as the "final arbiter" for determining the "acceptability" of antiracist actions:

> To what extent do our political strategies and alternative narratives about social difference succeed in alleviating campus racism, while at the same time managing *not to undercut* the efforts of other social groups to win self-definition? (p. 110)

It is noteworthy that this test—this principle—was putatively negotiated and agreed to (rationally?) among Ellsworth and individuals from a diversity of groups.

Some self-described postmodernist educational thinkers explicitly embrace general political principles. For example, Stanley Aronowitz and Henry Giroux (1991) acknowledge the force of the general sort of criticism advanced by Barber. In response, they call for a "critical" (versus "apolitical") postmodernism in which the "postmodern politics of difference" is combined with the "modernist struggle for justice, equality, and freedom" (p. 194).

This is all well and good, but there is a price to pay in theoretical coherence. For it is difficult to see how "critical postmodernism" can be systematically distinguished from the so-called metanarratives of Marxism and liberalism that it putatively rejects. The "modernist struggle" continues for Marxism and liberalism, and neither tradition has remained static. On the contrary, both have evolved so as to better cope with the "politics of difference," so emphasized in postmodernist analyses.[3]

Aronowitz and Giroux's (1991) idea of preserving important features of the modernist project is no doubt responsible in no small way for the vitriolic infighting that has broken out among postmodern educationists [and perhaps provides a clue to Ellsworth's (1992) overheated rhetoric].[4] Burbules and Rice (1991) characterize this dispute as one between "postmoderns" and "antimoderns." According to them, postmodern views (e.g., Aronowitz and Giroux's) suffer from a general lack of coherence and principled argument: "In place of such arguments we often find a highly charged rhetorical style that *asserts* the primacy of certain values or *condemns* their suppression without articulating why anyone not already sympathetic with their position ought to be so" (p. 398). Antimodern views (e.g., Ellsworth's) suffer from inconsistency, for "'rejected' modern principles often reappear in new guise" (p. 402).

"Antimoderns" certainly invite the charge of inconsistency. But whether they are simply employing hyperbole as a stratagem to take the unmasking of power relationships farther than "postmoderns" do is open to debate. In any case, the charge that Burbules and Rice (1991) advance against "postmodernism" applies to "antimodernism" as well. In general, postmodernism (and here I revert to common usage) is long on alerting us to the way in which claims to rationality can mask oppression but very short on telling us what is wrong with oppression and on providing guidance regarding what ought to be done about it (see also Bernstein, 1996; Gutmann, 1994; Lyon, 1994; and Taylor, 1994).

Decentering the Self

One important feature postmodernists attribute to the Marxist and liberal metanarratives is the commitment to an essential human self, a model to which all humankind should aspire and in terms of which all can be measured. Rationality and autonomy are its hallmarks, characteristics that are most readily identified with White European males of the ruling class. Postmodernists emphasize that models (identities) come in many forms, associated with race, class, and gender at the most general level, and are shaped by social and cultural contingencies. Identities must be seen as neither unified nor fixed but as various and continually "displaced/replaced" (e.g., Lather, 1991a). "De-centering" is the watchword: Political practice in which the universal Everyman presupposed by Marxist and liberal metanarratives occupies the center can function only to normalize and terrorize the many Others on the margins.

Once again the postmodernist critique undermines its own political project, in this case by rendering the question of who might be oppressed virtually impossible to answer. True, prescribing a particular voice for members of marginalized groups can be condescending, stereotyping, and oppressive. As Henry Louis Gates, Jr. (1992, chap. 10) remarks regarding the feeling he gets from his White colleagues in the academy: It is as if they were to provide him with a script and say, "Be oppositional—please. You look so cute when you're angry" (p. 185). But Gates also warns against taking decentering (what he calls the "rhetoric of dismantlement") too far:

> Foucault says, and let's take him at his word, that the "homosexual" as life form was invented sometime in the 19th century. Now, if there's no such thing as a homosexual, then homophobia, at least as directed toward people rather than acts, loses its rationale. But you can't respond to the discrimination against gay people by saying, "I'm sorry, I don't exist; you've got the wrong guy." (pp. 37–38)

Gates (1992) uses this example to identify a tension between what he calls "the imperatives of agency" and "the rhetoric of dismantlement." As I understand him, one can, following the postmodernists, conceive of homosexuality (or race, or gender) as "*only* a sociopolitical category," as he puts it. But—and this is the crux—that does not mean that such social categories ("constructions") are not *real* in their effects or that political practice can ignore this reality.

Acknowledging that members of social groups do not necessarily speak with one voice, acknowledging that identity is, as Cameron McCarthy (1993) puts it, "nonsynchronous," one is faced with the challenge to avoid a slide into the sort of radical dismantlement of group identity Gates warns against, which renders group oppression incoherent and reasoned political action to end it groundless. On the other hand, if one accepts that group identities do indeed exist, a serious commitment to recognize difference should not require that views expressed on contentious matters be uncritically and automatically accepted, on the grounds that unless one has "walked the walk," one must remain silent, that different canons of rationality are incommensurable, and so forth. Such a response to diversity results in a slide into a kind of group insularity that makes communication and negotiation across group differences impossible. It can also serve to romanticize oppressed groups, rendering them impervious to criticism regarding their own moral failings (e.g., Alston, 1995; West, 1992).

Postmodernist scholarship has done much to remind us of the ways in which persons can be silenced—terrorized—by an uncritical acceptance of the status quo and by blithely assuming an Enlightenment Everyman against which we can all agree to measure the worth of our lives. In my view, however, postmodernists are overly zealous in their deconstruction of notions such as rationality, equality, and the like, and are too sanguine about the implications. Their insights provide a starting point for reflecting about political and educational practice, but by no means an ending point.[5]

THE PARTICIPATORY EDUCATIONAL IDEAL

Iris Marion Young (1990a) formulates the problem as follows:

> We . . . must begin within the general historical and social conditions in which we exist. This means we must develop participatory democratic theory not on the assumption of an undifferentiated humanity, but rather on the assumption that there are group differences and that some groups are actually or potentially oppressed or disadvantaged.

She then responds with the following requirement:

> [A] democratic public . . . should provide mechanisms for the effective representation and recognition of the distinct voices and perspectives of those of its constituent groups that are oppressed or disadvantaged within it. (p. 128)

Young concedes to postmodernists that group differences are politically important, that they are rooted in historical contingency, and that they are associated with oppression and disadvantage. But she also concedes to melting pot thinkers that group differences can be adequately accommodated only to the extent that some democratic principles are shared across groups, across the "democratic public."

I think Young (1990a) is right about the general problem facing democratic theory, as well as the general solution. And both have important implications for education. On the one hand, no educational theory—liberal or otherwise—that aspires to prescribe the way in which education may serve to create and maintain a democratic society can avoid the commitment to engendering in students some shared beliefs, attitudes, and dispositions. On the other hand, what is to be shared should not be so culturally laden as to result in oppression or disadvantages for historically marginalized groups. To avoid this, the distinctive voices and perspectives of such groups must be recognized. This argument retraces some of my previous steps, and brings me once again to the participatory educational ideal.

I introduced the participatory ideal in Chapter 2 and then used it to reorient thinking about gender equality in Chapter 3. Here I extend and refine it in the process of working out my position on multicultural education. I use Amy Gutmann's (1987) "democratic threshold" as my point of departure.

Gutmann (1987) advances a position that places democracy at the center, and she fleshes out her "democratic threshold" accordingly. In particular, it requires that children be provided with an education that enables them to participate as equals in the democratic process of "conscious social reproduction." Failing to provide children with such an education undermines democracy itself. Among the aspects of the "democratic character" Gutmann envisages are values such as nonrepression, nondiscrimination, and tolerance, and dispositions to employ critical reasoning and to resolve disagreements nonviolently.

Like all thresholds, Gutmann's (1987) establishes a limit on the requirement of equalization. In her case, once the threshold is met, the "democratic authorization principle" permits, but does not require, further efforts at equalization. That is, if a community achieves the threshold for all its children and decides this is sufficient, then it has discharged its responsibility; if a community achieves the threshold for all its children and decides it wants to do more, then it is free to do so.

Gutmann (1987) takes us a considerable way toward specifying what the participatory educational ideal should require. However, her position needs revision in both content and procedures.

The guiding ideal for a democratic and just system of education should be broader in scope than Gutmann's (1987). She is correct to assign an obligation to the state to insure that its citizens are politically empowered in the way her threshold demands. Beyond this, however, any group differences in educational attainment that are systematically linked to goods such as employment, income, and health are prima facie unjust. Unless such inequalities are the result of morally relevant differences (religious belief, special talents, and conscious choice are examples), it is education's responsibility—as a public institution that importantly affects the lives of citizens—to intervene and level them (Strike, 1988).

Employment is especially germane here, for it plays a central role in individuals' lives, both as an intrinsic good and as an instrumental good that enables them to obtain other social goods. Thus one need not be narrowly focused on the vocational goals of education to believe that preparation for desirable employment ought to be included within the purview of the participatory ideal and to believe that failing to provide it fails to provide equality of educational opportunity. For example, it is safe to say that in the recent history of U.S. education, as many women as men have achieved Gutmann's democratic threshold. But, as described in Chapter 3, by virtue of various features of their context of choice, women still experience diminished educational opportunities overall in comparison to men (especially in math and science). As a result, they also experience diminished employment opportunities.

Gutmann (1987) uses her threshold to place a procedural constraint on what can be democratically decided. Nonetheless, specifying the threshold in concrete cases is a matter for democratic deliberation. These deliberations are not themselves totally unconstrained or totally a matter of majority rule. They are circumscribed by her two principles of "nonrepression" and "nondiscrimination," which she describes as follows:

> The principle of nonrepression prevents the state, and any group within it, from using education to restrict rational deliberation of competing conceptions of the good life and the good society. . . . Nondiscrimination extends the logic of nonrepression, since states and families can be selectively repressive by excluding entire groups of children from schooling or denying them an education conducive to deliberation among conceptions of the good life and the good society. (pp. 44–45)

The problem for Gutmann (1987) vis-à-vis multicultural education is that the general principle of "nonrepression" (of which "nondiscrimination" is a derivative) is too weak to adequately protect marginalized and oppressed groups in negotiating the participatory ideal. So far as I can tell, one could faithfully employ Gutmann's principles—allow everyone to have a say and make sure schools are equally open to all groups of children—and wind up with something very akin to Hirsch's (1988) "cultural literacy" as the threshold. To avoid this, a stronger principle—a principle of nonoppression—is required in order to protect groups that are threatened with maginalization and exclusion from meaningful democratic participation.[6] I will articulate such a principle in the next section. At this point it is sufficient to observe that Gutmann's own fundamental premise demands that constraints on democratic decision-making are justified insofar as they are required in democracy's own name.

The Virtue of Recognition

Changing from the principle of nonrepression to the principle of nonoppresssion has the consequence of changing the way "democratic character" should be understood. The virtue of tolerance, included in Gutmann's (1987) explication of democratic character, parallels her principle of nonrepression and is likewise too weak. Merely tolerating or "putting up with" alternative and dissenting views is insufficient. For, once heard, they can be all too easily dismissed. By contrast, the virtue of "recognition" parallels the principle of nonoppression and is likewise more demanding in its requirements.

Charles Taylor (1995) identifies recognition with the presumption that the contributions of diverse cultures have equal worth. For him, only ethnocentric arrogance could justify the view that the traditional Western canon is the sole source of artistic and intellectual merit. Indeed, Westerners are in no position even to judge the contribution of other cultures until they have taken a long, hard look at them and have achieved the kind of understanding, the kind of "fusion of horizons," required to evaluate them properly. This is not to say that the presumption cannot prove over time to have been unwarranted. Moreover, some cultures and cultural phases can be preempted from the presumption at the outset. Nazi Germany seems an obvious example.

Inasmuch as he seeks to recognize marginalized and oppressed groups but to avoid the nihilistic excesses of postmodernism (what he calls the "neo-Nietzschean standpoint"), Taylor (1994) is trying to accomplish the same thing I am. But the aim that he adopts for multicultural education is too narrow, focusing exclusively on the potential contribution that the products of diverse cultures can make to a revised canon. Studying cultures different from one's own, no doubt, naturally results in some increased understanding and appreciation. If it did not—if it resulted in a view of another culture as, say, an intellectual and moral abomination—it is hard to imagine how recognition could be fostered. Increased understanding and appreciation, however, need not and probably cannot go to the extreme of a "fusion of horizons," even where this is acknowledged as an accomplishment that, as Taylor says, is "very far away." Indeed, the idea of fusing horizons entails a kind of utopian-communitarianism in which group distinctiveness vanishes. In practice, historically marginalized groups would be those most saddled with the burden to fuse (assimilate?)—and most vulnerable to continued oppression.

A revised canon is not the only educational goal to be served by multicultural education, after all, or even the most important one. Multicultural education should, as Susan Wolf (1994) says, make it possible for us to "come to recognize ourselves as a multicultural community and so to recognize and respect the members of that community in all our diversity" (p. 83). Perhaps where a relatively small number of cultural groups are involved, the goals of fostering the virtue of recognition and reformulating the canon can significantly dovetail. But given the huge number of cultural groups represented in the U.S. public schools,[7] only a small portion could find their way into a revised canon. Reformulating the canon thus loses salience because many cultures exist whose study could foster the virtue of recognition. It also becomes counterproductive because the criterion of worth of contribution would unavoidably exclude certain cultural groups that attend U.S. public schools and therefore would deny them recognition.

I don't want to overstate the case against the value of a revised canon, particularly were it to include comprehensive and faithful treatments of important but neglected groups in U.S. history, such as Native Americans, African Americans, and Mexican Americans.[8] Whatever canon is negotiated, however, it should be *partial*, which is to say that it should leave considerable room for individual schools to afford genuine recognition to the particular cultural groups they serve and, at the same time, to foster the virtue of recognition in others. Accordingly, the partial canon should be filled out in a way attuned to the cultural makeup of local communities.[9]

The Principle of Nonoppression

To reiterate, because the principle of nonrepression places too weak a procedural constraint on the process of negotiating the curriculum to protect oppressed groups adequately, it needs to be supplanted with a principle of nonoppression. The principle of nonoppression can be implemented either formally or informally. A formal implementation requires establishing new rules and procedures that guarantee all groups are genuinely recognized. Special rights for oppressed groups is a proposal in this vein that is currently garnering significant attention among political theorists.[10] By contrast, an informal implementation foregoes measures such as group rights in favor trusting the good will of those engaged in decision-making to interpret the rules and procedures already in place so as to insure that recognition occurs.[11] In my view, formalized measures are required to realize a just society under present historical conditions, but the difficult task of defending this claim is not something I want to undertake here. I limit myself to the more modest task of articulating how, when observed, the principle of nonoppression can foster genuine democratic negotiation, whatever its precise form of implementation might be.

If all groups are permitted merely to express their views, negotiations devolve into "special interests" bargaining and the idea of special protections goes by the boards (Young, 1990a). Whether employed formally or informally, then, the principle of nonoppression requires identifying groups that qualify as oppressed and that therefore can legitimately claim special protections.

Young (1990a) identifies five forms of oppression that serve to make this identification possible: exploitation, marginalization, powerlessness, cultural imperialism, and violence. These forms overlap and crisscross in complex ways, but they can be nonetheless roughly distinguished. Briefly, exploitation, marginalization, and powerlessness are forms of oppression associated with different effects of the economic system. Cultural imperialism is a form of oppression associated with the imposition of the cultural meanings of the dominant group on all groups. Violence is a form of oppression associated with the attitudes and practices that cultural imperialism sanctions.

Schooling has a responsibility to help eliminate each of these forms of oppression. Cultural imperialism, however, is probably the most far reaching and, along with violence, the form most directly under the control of schools. I thus focus on these two forms, but especially cultural imperialism. Expanding the arena of "multiculturalism" and "multicultural education" in a way that has become commonplace, that is, well beyond language, ethnicity, and nationality, I consider three contrasting sets of claims with respect to the oppressiveness of public education: gay and lesbian youth versus Christian fundamentalists, autonomous versus immigrant versus castelike minorities,[12] and integrationists versus separatists. Taken together, these contrasts should help clarify when groups' claims to being oppressed by schooling are well-founded and what the response to such claims should be.

CONTRAST 1: GAY AND LESBIAN YOUTH VERSUS CHRISTIAN FUNDAMENTALISTS. The collateral learning associated with what schools leave out of their curricula is often as important as (if not more important than) the learning associated with what is included. It is thus significant that the public school curriculum largely excludes discussion of gay and lesbian issues and gay and lesbian role models. It is also significant that when homosexuality is addressed, it is typically characterized as a pathology for which persons should seek help. Richard Friend (1993) labels these two features of schooling, respectively, "systematic exclusion" and "systematic inclusion" and contends that they work in tandem to institutionalize heterosexism. In this way, gay and lesbian youth suffer from cultural imperialism, which is, in turn, implicated in violence against them. Indeed, violence against gay and lesbian youth is the highest of any group and is associated with much higher than average rates of suicide, truancy, and dropping out. Friend observes that gay and lesbian youth who manage to avoid these problems do so by adopting various strategies that overtly embrace cultural imperialism (heterosexism), such as accommodation (e.g., telling "fag" jokes) or heterosexual overcompensation (e.g., maintaining a sexual relationship with a member of the opposite sex).

The principle of nonoppression provides straightforward guidance here: It requires eliminating Friend's (1993) "systematic inclusion" and "systematic exclusion" from the curriculum. It also requires reshaping practice so as to eliminate violence, in both its overt and its subtle (as well as not so subtle) verbal forms.

If it is to perform its function, the principle of nonoppression must be capable of distinguishing cases like this from cases that do not qualify for the protections it provides. Christian fundamentalist reformers (at least the vocal and well-known ones) provide an example of the latter. Although it would be odd for them to promote multiculturalism or to use the language of oppression, they nonetheless make what amounts to the claim that they are victimized by cultural imperialism. They also demand recognition.

Where Christian fundamentalists (or any religious groups, for that matter) are systematically denied recognition within the public schools, they have the makings of a legitimate grievance. Furthermore, given the importance that religion plays in so many peoples' lives, failing to incorporate it in a substantive way into schooling circumvents the virtue of recognition and compromises the education of everyone.[13]

Still, not all claims of oppression are on a par. Schools are on solid ground insofar as the oppression Christian fundamentalists experience takes the form of a refusal by schools to recognize the doctrinaire posture of "dominion" that, as Pat Robertson would have it, affords recognition only to those "who believe the Judeo-Christian values" (in Cox, 1995, p. 66). For nonoppression is rooted in the requirements of democracy. It must be both applied to and observed by all who make up a political community, which is to say it must be reciprocal. The problem with Christian fundamentalist reformers is that they refuse to embrace reciprocity: They are cultural imperialists who want recognition only for themselves.

The stance of Christian fundamentalist reformers thus serves to raise the perennial question for liberal theorists of education of how to respond to the intolerant. Briefly, to live up to its principles, a liberal democracy must maintain as neutral a position as possible regarding the views of the good its citizens are free to adopt. Even the most obnoxious world views, like those of neo-Nazis, for instance, are permitted, so long as their purveyors restrict themselves to nonviolent activities and pose no serious threat to survival of democracy. Given this reasoning, it is better on balance to permit the avowal of such world views than to try to define what views are impermissible and to enforce sanctions against them. Furthermore, the intolerant might very well learn a useful lesson from the example set by an overall tolerant society (e.g., Rawls, 1971).

But permitting undemocratic, intolerant, oppressive world views is different from encouraging them. Indeed, it is permissible, if not obligatory, to do just the opposite. This applies especially to schooling, because it plays (or should play) such a crucial role in forming democratic character. To the extent that Christian fundamentalist reformers reject this role, it is legitimate to require them to pay for private schools out of their own pockets and, even then, to also impose certain restrictions on the schools they create, both in the name of democracy and in the name of their children's welfare.

CONTRAST 2: AUTONOMOUS VERSUS IMMIGRANT VERSUS CASTELIKE MINORITIES. Although usually not as starkly as in the case of gay and lesbian youth, numerous other groups within the schools also qualify as oppressed in terms of cultural imperialism and violence: for instance, African Americans, Mexican Americans, Puerto Ricans, Native Americans, Jews, Arabs, Asians, Southeast Asians, girls and women, the physically and mentally disabled, and certain religious groups. And they, too, are often faced with the dilemma of being or trying to be someone they are not or suffering the consequences.

Although it would be wrong-headed to try to develop a precise ranking of oppressed groups, there are, nonetheless, important differences in the moral status of the demands they make and, accordingly, in what the response of a democratic society should be. These differences are captured by the distinction John Ogbu and Maria Matute-Bianchi (1986) make among autonomous, immigrant, and castelike minorities.

Autonomous minorities. An example of an autonomous minority is the Amish. Like the Christian fundamentalist reformers considered in the previous section, the Amish reject the participatory educational ideal as a threat to their way of life. Both wish to determine their own view of educational opportunities worth wanting, consistent with their cultural (particularly religious) sensibilities. But unlike Christian fundamentalist reformers, the Amish are separatists who neither appeal to the state to provide for community members' welfare nor attempt to influence public education. And this makes their case quite different.

Because the Amish do not seek state support for their schools and do not seek to promote cultural imperialism through the vehicle of the public schools, the state has a greater obligation to permit the Amish to opt out of the requirements of the participatory ideal in the name of nonoppression than it does in the case of Christian fundamentalists. Because the state's interests in promoting democratic and employable citizens remain legitimate, the question is one of balance. Although their form of schooling is antidemocratic, the Amish exhibit no tendency to try to implement it beyond the bounds of their communities, and although their schooling fails to prepare children for participation in a modern economy, the Amish don't aspire to such participation. Their communities are largely self-sufficient.[14]

Even when the interests of the state are set aside, however, a worry nonetheless exists (a worry that applies to Christian fundamentalist children as well) that the interests of Amish children themselves are compromised by the kind and amount of schooling they receive (Gutmann, 1987). In particular, Amish schooling fails to provide the intellectual skills and knowledge that enable persons to decide for themselves what kind of lives to lead. Worse, it may permanently block the possibility of acquiring them. It thus sacrifices the cherished ideal of autonomy (cherished by liberals at least) to the interests of the community.

So far as I can tell, this conundrum has no altogether satisfactory solution. Liberals can either (uneasily) advocate denying the right to the Amish to educate their children in a way consistent with their community norms and values, in the name of individual autonomy, or, as I do (also uneasily), advocate affording them this right, in the name of a reasonable political compromise.[15]

Immigrant minorities. An example of an immigrant minority is Chinese Americans. According to Ogbu and Matute-Bianchi (1986), Chinese Americans entered the United States voluntarily and exhibit an "alternation model of behavior," whereby they are neither assimilated into nor reject the mainstream U.S. culture reflected in the public schools. Instead, they move back and forth between cultures as circumstances dictate.

Because they embrace participating in the broad political-economic community, groups such as Chinese Americans seem to have much less reason to object to the participatory educational ideal than do autonomous minorities such as the Amish. For, through their own devices, they manage to keep their cultural identity intact. Of course, this is not to suggest that they are not and have not been oppressed by the public schools, or that they have no legitimate grievances. Consider the 1886 unanimous resolution of the San Francisco School Board:

> No principal, teacher or employee of the Public Schools Department shall employ, patronize, aid or encourage the Chinese in any way, but shall do all in their power to legally promote their removal from this coast and discourage further immigration. (in Baron, 1990, p. 133)

However oppressive their treatment at the hands of public schools, the response of Chinese Americans has been to seek meaningful inclusion, not to remain separate. The celebrated *Lau v. Nichols* (1974) case attests to this. The Chinese American plaintiffs sued to gain their children access to the curriculum of the public schools in the language the children understood, not because they perceived the cultural content of the existing curriculum as a threat to their own culture.

Castelike minorities. Castelike minorities include groups such as African Americans, Mexican Americans, and Native Americans. Unlike autonomous minorities, they typically aspire to participate in the broader political-economic community; unlike immigrant minorities, they became a part of the political-economic community involuntarily. Because of their peculiar circumstances, rather than adopting the separatist strategy of the Amish or the alternation strategy of Chinese Americans, castelike minorities have adopted an "oppositional" strategy to preserve (or create) their cultural identity. Such a strategy typically entails poor school performance, because doing well in school requires accepting the values of the dominant culture to which castelike minorities are in opposition.

Of the three kinds of minorities considered, castelike minorities feel oppression most in the form of cultural imperialism. Unlike the Amish, they attend public schools; unlike Chinese Americans, they fare poorly there and are unwilling or unable to adopt the predominant norms. The oppositional behavior they display is not a deliberate strategy and is often self-defeating. It results from the perception (often accurate) that unless one is a member of the dominant culture, doing well in school will not result in the benefits that are promised, and from the perception (again, often accurate) that one must allow one's behavior and identity to be defined in terms of the dominant culture (e.g., by "acting White") in order to do well.

An obligation clearly exists to afford recognition to autonomous and immigrant minorities, but this obligation is especially exacting with respect to castelike minorities. Because they became subjects of U.S. government through capture and conquest, and were subsequently subjected to efforts to demolish their cultures—either directly, through intense control of their education and family life, indirectly, through powerful influences toward Americanization, or both—their history gives them a special moral claim. Schooling is deeply implicated in this history, and, accordingly, has a corresponding special obligation.[16]

CONTRAST 3: INTEGRATIONISM VERSUS SEPARATISM. In the celebrated *Brown v. Board of Education* (1954) decision, the Supreme Court reasoned that racially segregated schools are "inherently unequal" because of the damage they do to the self-respect of African Americans and because of the consequences this has on African Americans' school performance. This reasoning was subsequently extended to ethnic groups such as Mexican Americans in *Keyes v. School District No. 1* (1973) and is implicated in laws to promote equality of educational opportunity for linguistic minorities, girls and women, and people with disabilities as well (e.g., Salamone, 1986).

Of course, serious questions have been raised about this integrationist line of reasoning (e.g., Kymlicka, 1991) and, contra *Brown*, "separate but equal" has been resurrected as a distributive principle. Indeed, if anything, it is integration that is "inherently unequal," because it invariably results in cultural imperialism. This is the kind of argument that undergirds, for example, all-male Afrocentric academies and all-girl classrooms and schools.

The disagreement between integrationists and separatists has more to do with the means by which to respond to oppressive schooling than with either identifying what groups it affects or embracing the obligation to end it. To be sure, important differences exist between the social situation and social theory that prevailed in 1954 and those that prevail today. Nonetheless, the reasoning of *Brown* is still germane and is echoed in current calls to recognize the cultural identities of diverse groups. Consider how cultural imperialism threatens self-respect and how it is, in turn, implicated in oppositional behavior. The problem is that integration efforts have been consistently half-hearted (Gutmann, 1987; Shofield, 1991). Here it is useful to conceive of varieties of integration in parallel to my three interpretations of equality of educational opportunity.

Formal integration efforts include measures such as magnet schools and busing. Their aim is limited to mixing diverse groups; they make no effort to renegotiate the norms, practices, and curricula of schools accordingly. The results have not been encouraging (Salamone, 1986; Shofield, 1991), and segregation often reemerges *within* schools through practices such as tracking (an issue considered in detail in Chapter 5). *Compensatory* integration efforts go beyond formal efforts by attempting to redress past wrongs and to compensate for disadvantages. They are exemplified by programs such as bilingual education, special education, free school lunches, Title I, and the like. Like formal efforts, however, they leave the existing norms, practices, and curricula largely in place. Consequently, they do little to afford recognition to the groups they seek to benefit, and the kinds of opportunity costs they exact—particularly in terms of self-identity—can be great. Whole-hearted, *participatory* integration efforts—efforts that truly recognize diverse groups as dictated by the participatory ideal—have yet to be tried.

In the more than forty years since *Brown*, initial progress has been followed by decades of backsliding (Kozol, 1991). But it is difficult to see how separatism is the solution. In my view, it is more likely to exacerbate the problem than to solve it. For separatism largely walks away from the problem of fostering democratic virtues through schooling, leaving these to take care of themselves. As a consequence, it threatens to impede progress toward a more democratic and just society by failing to challenge current gender and race relations, or even by reinforcing them (e.g., Alston, 1995; Connell, 1993). Furthermore, as a practical matter, not nearly enough diversity exists in the pool of teachers to staff a system of separate but equal schools (Kozol, 1993). Finally, how else, post-*Brown*, can separatism be implemented except through the mechanism of school choice? As I argue in Chapter 7, school choice proposals are unlikely to satisfy the ''but equal'' requirement and, in general, pose a serious threat to schooling for democratic participation.

CONCLUSION

The end of this chapter marks the end of a line of argument that has spanned the last several chapters. The next three chapters, on segregation, testing, and choice, largely presuppose the analyses I have provided so far.

Looking back, I introduced the participatory educational ideal in Chapter 2 and located it within the broader terrain of liberal political theory. I further refined it in Chapter 3, paying special attention to the limitations of the "distributive paradigm" of justice and how these might be overcome with a participatory (transformational) view that resolves the apparent conflict between the "political" and "educational" aims of schooling. I used the issue of gender equality and the work of certain feminists for this intermediate step. I also examined gender equality as an important topic in its own right.

Multicultural education is an important topic in its own right as well. Indeed, under a not uncommon interpretation, it may be seen as subsuming gender equality. This is particularly so where the complexity of gender is appreciated, including how it interacts with other social categories to yield unique kinds of identities. This helps explain why I used the issue of multicultural education to round out the participatory educational ideal.

Built upon Gutmann's (1987) "democratic threshold," the participatory educational ideal is nonetheless distinguished from it by two key elements: the virtue of recognition and the principle of nonoppression. "Recognition," as I use it, requires appreciating characteristics such as race, ethnicity, gender, culture, language, religion, and sexual orientation as central to persons' identities. It also requires recognizing the injustice of coercing persons with the trade-off—the one faced by Richard Rodriguez, Delbert Thunderwolf, and Jo Vega—of either giving up who they are or forgoing full membership in the democratic public and the other social goods that go with it. Where the virtue of recognition is not widely shared by the members of group-differentiated societies, which almost all modern societies are, it is difficult to imagine how a genuine democracy can exist.

The principle of nonoppression functions to define injustice and to mediate among the claims of different groups. It is an ineluctable fact that differences in power and privilege are real and are rooted in group membership. Where no principled way exists to respond to this fact, it is likewise difficult to imagine a genuine democracy.

The view I have developed in the last three chapters, then, concedes to critics of liberalism that distributive justice and democracy are inseparable, that the worth of what is to be distributed must itself be open to negotiation. In this vein, and against melting pot thinkers, I agree with postmodernists that the question of what educational opportunities are universally—equally—worth wanting has to be put on the table. But against postmodernists, I agree with melting pot thinkers that some such educational opportunities are required to render the quest for just and democratic schooling coherent.

CHAPTER 5

Segregation

[I]n the field of public education the doctrine of "separate but equal" has no place. Separate educational facilities are inherently unequal.
—Brown v. Board of Education

Segregation in the U.S. public schools takes two general forms: between schools and within schools. As the names suggest, between-school segregation assigns students to different schools (e.g., on the basis of race), whereas within-school segregation assigns students to different curricular options within the same school (e.g., on the basis of test scores). Both forms of segregation compromise equality of educational opportunity in significant ways. I begin with a few observations about between-school segregation. I then turn to within-school segregation, the primary focus of this chapter.

BETWEEN-SCHOOL SEGREGATION

The *Brown* decision outlawed the de jure form of between-school segregation, particularly that based on race (*Brown v. Board of Education*, 1954). But de facto between-school segregation has continued largely unchecked (Kozol, 1991; Shofield, 1991), and it is subject to criticisms very similar to those that led the Supreme Court to ban de jure segregation.

In *Brown*, the U.S. Supreme Court struck down the "separate but equal" principle articulated some 50 years earlier in *Plessy v. Ferguson* (1896). An important part of the argument was that even if, contrary to fact, resources were distributed equally among racially segregated schools, legally sanctioned segregation so stigmatizes and demoralizes segregated groups as to permanently disadvantage them. As things now stand, the "but equal" clause is so far from being satisfied as to be moot. Nonetheless, an important part of the argument of the Supreme Court still applies. In addition to the obvious consequences of blatantly unequal resources, students at the bottom of the resource heap (typically racial and ethnic minorities) can't help but get the message that they and theirs are not worth much in the eyes of society (Kozol, 1991). That their segregation is pervasive, deep-rooted, and staunchly defended seems no less likely to permanently demoralize and disadvantage them than requiring it by law.

Much could be said about between-school segregation, particularly in light of the separatist movement that, in effect, seeks to breathe life back into the separate but equal principle. I touched on my reservations about separatism in the previous chapter on multiculturalism, and I introduce several new ones in the subsequent chapter on choice. In the remainder of this chapter, I set this issue aside.

WITHIN-SCHOOL SEGREGATION

Within-school segregation is associated primarily with differentiating the curriculum according to academic talent. The precise form it takes varies widely, but the general scheme is as follows: At one extreme is special education, at the other extreme is gifted education, and in the middle are various "tracks" (e.g., college preparatory, general, and vocational).[1] I begin my analysis with tracking.

Tracking

Two primary rationales are provided for tracking: best interests and utilitarian. The best interests rationale sees tracking as the way to provide the best and most appropriate education for everyone. Mixing children of different talents, so the argument goes, bores the most talented and swamps and humiliates the least, reducing learning in each case.[2] Thus grouping students with respect to ability and differentiating the curriculum accordingly is in the best interests of all students and, happily, renders the difficult question of who must sacrifice misconceived.

The best interests rationale runs into serious difficulty in light of the empirical research on tracking. Although the topic has been and continues to be highly contentious, there seems little question that tracking does indeed require some trade-offs. In perhaps the most intensive and influential research of its kind, Jeannie Oakes (1985) concluded that tracking unequivocally compromises the educational opportunities experienced by students in low tracks. Its effect on middle-, and especially higher, track students, she found, were less clear.

If Oakes (1985) is right, tracking denies low-track students even formal equality of educational opportunity (the weakest and most inadequate kind from among the three I have distinguished). In comparison to those enjoyed by higher track students, the "inputs" experienced by lower track students are far from equal. Among other inequalities, lower track students are taught by inferior teachers, exposed to inferior curriculum materials, and subject to inferior classroom environments. In such arrangements, then, and contrary to the best interests rationale, tracking does indeed trade off opportunities.

There may be a way to defend the best interests rationale in the face of the evidence Oakes (1985) provides. In particular, the sort of trade-off described would be warranted (or at least would be much more defensible) if lower track students proved incapable of taking advantage of improved educational opportunities (in the form of "inputs"), whereas higher track students did not. Given this premise, untracked curriculum arrangements would have no positive effects on students who would otherwise be in lower tracks but would serve to diminish the opportunities of students who would otherwise be in higher tracks. Only envy and the perversity of dragging everyone down in the name of equality would support forgoing tracking if this premise is true.

Now, there is no a priori reason why this cannot be the way things work. On the contrary, many people no doubt intuit that it is futile and wasteful to pour educational resources into the academically less talented. But this intuition rests on quite shaky ground. Prominent empirical researchers on both sides of the tracking debate agree that, in practice, untracked arrangements benefit students who would otherwise be in lower tracks and exact some sacrifice from students who would otherwise be in higher tracks; tracked arrangements do the reverse (Hallinan, 1994b; Oakes, 1994).

This points in the direction of the utilitarian rationale for tracking, which concedes the unavoidability of trade-offs but invokes its principle of maximizing benefit to justify certain ways of making them.[3] It sees tracking as the rational response to differences in ability. With an eye toward developing "human capital" to the fullest, it sanctions distributing a disproportionate share of educational resources to the most promising students. The alternative is "dumbing down" the curriculum in a way that requires the most talented to sacrifice in deference to equalizing the prospects of the slow and mediocre (Murray & Herrnstein, 1994, chaps. 17 and 18). This ultimately compromises the health of the nation, particularly with respect to economic competitiveness.

The general criticism of utilitarianism's conception of equality of educational opportunity advanced in Chapter 2 applies quite straightforwardly to the utilitarian rationale for tracking. Recall that liberal-egalitarian critics of utilitarianism insist on a principled commitment to equality of educational opportunity with the first and foremost requirement to insure that everyone obtains a "fair share" of education (fleshed out in the last chapter in terms of the participatory educational ideal). Because utilitarianism lacks such a commitment, it renders equality of educational opportunity all too vulnerable. In the case of tracking (which for present purposes may be assumed to maximize benefits, say, by producing more and better engineers and scientists), utilitarianism sanctions an arrangement in which the least advantaged (i.e., those in the low tracks) receive an inferior education in order that the most advantaged (i.e., those in the high tracks) may receive a superior one. The fact that tracking is so often associated with differential benefits according to race, class, and gender (Oakes, 1990; Oakes, Ormseth, Bell, & Camp, 1990) only renders the injustice more acute.

The tracking debate typically founders about here—on claims and counterclaims about whether tracking (or de-tracking, as the case may be) entails trading the benefits of some students for the benefits of others and, if so, how this might be justified. To be sure, these questions cannot be avoided altogether. But they should not be addressed as they so often are: as if things could not be otherwise, as if current funding, teaching practices, and curricula—the basis for most empirical research conclusions on tracking—were set in stone.[4]

Consider funding. The question of a just distribution clearly turns on how trade-offs are made *given* a certain amount to be distributed, both between and within schools. But the answer to this question unavoidably turns on the further question—which empirical studies of tracking so often neglect—of what the total available amount is. When total educational funding is far too low, as I believe it is,[5] difficult trade-offs are forced. In turn, when not all children can receive an adequate education, it makes sense in the name of efficiency to distribute resources to those students who will yield the "greatest return on investment." It makes sense, in other words, to distribute resources in favor of the most talented. Of course, short of unlimited funding, the problem of trade-offs cannot be eliminated altogether. On the other hand, its acuteness could surely be diminished were funding significantly increased.

Consider the related question of teaching practices. Increased funding would help reduce the pressures that the zero-sum game of inadequate funding creates. Among other benefits, increased funding would make possible reductions in class size as well as better training, salaries, and working conditions for teachers. Under the right conditions—the kind of conditions increased funding makes possible—a nontracked arrangement can be practiced in a way that significantly sacrifices the benefits of no one (Oakes et al., 1990).

Finally, consider curricula. In my view, large and fundamental questions arise here—about democracy, justice, and equality of educational opportunity—that are all but ignored in the way the debate about tracking is most often framed. Typically, formal opportunities, achievement, and self-esteem provide the data from which conclusions are drawn regarding who benefits from and who is harmed by tracked arrangements. The tacit assumption is that, for the most part, all is well with the present curriculum. Under this assumption, equality of opportunity is to be achieved either by equalizing the quantity of this curriculum to which different students are exposed (where inputs are the criterion) or by equalizing the quantity they master (where outcomes are the criterion). (Self-esteem is tacked on as a largely ancillary consideration.)

Because the present curriculum so neglects the importance of fostering the virtue of recognition, as well as democratic participation more generally, the above framework forces the question of whether to track into the "distributive paradigm" (described in Chapter 3). That is, the question must be entertained primarily or exclusively in terms of trade-offs among students' individual interests in mastering the curriculum.

Although I don't want to dismiss altogether the way of looking at tracking associated with the "distributive paradigm," this perspective is clearly too narrow. Tracking ought to be viewed from a broader perspective, one more attuned to the demands of democracy and justice.

Michael Walzer (1983) observes that

> children are each other's resources: comrades and rivals, challenging one another, helping one another, forming what well may be the crucial friendships of their adult lives. The content of the curriculum is probably less important than the human environment within which it is taught. (p. 215)

Walzer (1983) is surely getting at something more far-reaching than the idea that children can (should) help one another to master the traditional "academic" curriculum. At least two more fundamental ideas may be extracted from his observation: one associated most closely with distributive justice and the other most closely with democracy.

First, social cooperation is deeply implicated in defining and rewarding talents. Too often people seem to want to take complete credit for the talents they and theirs possess, and resent being called upon to make what they view as sacrifices for the benefit of others. Those who hold this view believe that providing especially desirable education in the form of high tracks for the talented is only what the talented deserve. One obvious problem with this view is that people are advantaged or disadvantaged by contingencies over which they have no control, by what John Rawls (1971) calls the natural and social "lotteries." A related but less obvious problem is that the talents individuals possess do not intrinsically possess or lack value but depend for their worth on the social circumstances in which they are embedded (Dworkin, 1977). Take computer software designers, and consider the high degree of social cooperation required for them to both develop and find use for their talents. Then compare their talents with those valued and rewarded in Spartan or Amish society. It is only by ignoring the relevance of social contingency in both its more and less obvious forms that complaints about the alleged sacrifices required of the talented in foregoing tracking could gain the force they have.

Second, certain human characteristics can be realized only through active engagement in social cooperation (e.g., Taylor, 1989); the democratic virtue of recognition (discussed in detail in Chapter 4) is an especially good example. In particular, social cooperation should not be viewed as a mere means to foster "academic" achievement. True, it can be realized within groups that are relatively insulated from one another, say, high tracks versus low tracks. But if public education is going to take promoting democracy seriously, it is going to have to take what this requires seriously as well. This creates a strong presumption against school segregation in all its forms, for it is unlikely that students segregated into tracks can still learn to afford recognition to those quite different from themselves, particularly in light of the status differences that such segregation creates (Oakes, 1985). This is not an argument for jettisoning curriculum differentiation per se, on the model of the *Paideia Proposal* (1982), for example. Rather, it is an argument for framing the questions of how to justify curriculum differentiation and identify its acceptable forms in a different way.

In light of the arguments of Chapters 2 through 4, little by way of additional conceptual tools is required to tackle these questions. Consistent with the central place occupied by the participatory educational ideal, the first responsibility of public schooling is to educate its students for democratic participation. Contrary to the opinion of traditionalists who bother to take the democratic aims of public education seriously (and not all do), democratic citizenship won't magically take care of itself by providing different students with as much of the traditional liberal arts curriculum as they are willing and able to master.[6] What is more, this kind of tracking by attrition, as it might be called, insures that many public school students will fail (Noddings, 1992).

To be sure, some traditional educational goals should be adopted for all K–12 students—basic literacy and numeracy, for instance, as well as some literature, some art, some history, some science, some geography, and so forth. But that the best way to fill out these "somes" is by appeal to the liberal arts is not self-evident, for the value of the traditional liberal arts is not self-evident either (an argument I develop further in Chapter 6). The liberal arts are anchored in traditionalism and intellectualism. That they can serve by themselves to foster democracy is but an unexamined article of faith.

The participatory educational ideal is, by contrast, self-consciously anchored in democracy. The universal aims it incorporates—the virtue of recognition, the capacity for democratic deliberation, and the prospect of gainful employment, for instance—are rooted in education for democracy. Beyond these general requirements, the participatory ideal is quite congenial to marked curriculum differentiation. The crucial proviso, however, is that curriculum differentiation be driven by students' interests, not by the imperative to sort them into categories so as to best round out a "human capital portfolio."[7]

This idea, of course, is not new. John Dewey is no doubt its best known advocate, and it has recently been rejuvenated by theorists such as Nel Noddings and Jane Roland Martin (who contribute substantially to the argument against the liberal arts I develop in Chapter 6). This perspective should not be identified (as it so often has been in the case of Dewey) with an indulgent "child-centered" approach, in which the rash and immature judgments of children are permitted to hold sway. Especially in the early grades, it is permissible—indeed, it is required—for educators to inculcate democratic character as well as to push, pull, and cajole children in the direction of other, more traditional educational ends. Gradually, however, as children age and mature, and as the general requirements of the participatory ideal are satisfied, they should be permitted to forego uniform curriculum requirements and to exercise increasing discretion in what interests they wish to develop. Because talents and interests typically go hand-in-hand, it is unlikely that the less talented in a given area would often choose to pursue something they are not good at and thereby drag down the more talented in that area. In any case, there comes a time in the majority of students' lives, including those students whose interests are primarily intellectual, when it is fruitless and counterproductive to coerce them in directions they would rather not go.[8]

Gifted Education

Gifted education falls under the rubric "exceptionality," which also includes special education. Unlike special education, however, gifted education is not required by federal law. Nonetheless, as of 1990, 26 states and trust territories required gifted programs, and all but 6 had some form of state support for gifted programs or legislation encouraging local districts to provide them (U.S. Department of Education, 1995).

Versions of the same two rationales used to support tracking are also used to support gifted education: utilitarian and best interests.[9] The utilitarian rationale is very much the same as for tracking. Gifted education (a super high track, as it were) is required to develop the skills of the most talented, so that they can assume the reins of leadership, increase the nation's economic competitiveness, and generally improve our lot.

> [W]e . . . must challenge our top performing students to greater heights if our nation is to achieve a world-class educational system. In order to make economic strides, America must rely on its top-performing students to provide leadership—in mathematics, science, writing, politics, dance, art, business, history, health, and other human pursuits. (U.S. Department of Education, 1995, p. 1)

Though in somewhat more muted language (the reference is to a "quiet crisis" rather than an "act of war"), the arguments in this vein echo the rhetoric that has been with us since the publication of *A Nation at Risk* (1983), and they are vulnerable to the same criticisms against utilitarian rationales that I have just reiterated with respect to tracking. On the other hand, certain peculiarities of gifted education bring several difficulties into sharper relief.

Utilitarian rationales in general require accurate predictions of what policies and practices will maximize benefits. In the case of the utilitarian rationale for gifted education, a reasonably accurate method is needed to predict which children will ultimately make extraordinary contributions to society. But the criteria used to place children in gifted education do not supply this information (Bull, 1985). Despite concerted efforts to zero in on the construct (including, for instance, distinguishing among the "highly," "severely," "profoundly," and "exotic" gifted), at best no correlation exists between identification criteria and adult giftedness, and at worst the correlation is negative (Richert, 1991). Gifted education programs thus may be labeled unjust insofar as they provide extra benefits to certain children on irrelevant grounds. And this criticism gains force to the extent that the identification of giftedness is so often associated with race, gender, and class (a point I return to below).

In a kind of "Catch-22," solving this problem would generate another one, perhaps more serious. Estimates of the number of gifted children vary from 3–5% (U.S. Department of Education, 1995) to 3–9% (Gallagher & Gallagher, 1994) to 1–15% (Sapon-Shevin, 1994). The vast range here provides a clue to just how nebulous the construct of giftedness is. Clearly, a much smaller proportion of individuals than provided in any of these estimates, substantially less than 0.1% is my bet, make extraordinary contributions to society. If these truly gifted children could be picked out, then the injustice described above could be eliminated. But a consistent application of the utilitarian rationale would require distributing extra educational resources only to these truly gifted and, accordingly, would entail drastically reducing the number of children who currently qualify for gifted programs. The Catch-22 is that this would doom gifted education by destroying its constituency.

The best interests rationale for gifted education is modified from the form it takes with respect to tracking (that all students' interests are served) to focus specifically on the interests of the gifted, trading on a purported parallel with special education. That is, gifted children, like children with disabilities, are deemed a special needs population (as "exceptional"), who require a specially tailored curriculum to enjoy equality of educational opportunity.

This rationale for gifted education is strained at best. It seems no coincidence that the alleged special needs of gifted students are routinely met with what looks to all the world like superior educational opportunities. Gifted programs typically help those fortunate enough to be in them to accumulate more "cultural capital" and to accumulate it faster.This is accomplished by accelerating gifted students through the K–12 curriculum; by permitting them to take high school courses while they are still in middle school and university courses while they are still in high school; by providing the learning conditions that facilitate this, such as small class sizes; by emphasizing autonomous thinking and "higher order" skills; and by providing superior teachers, curriculum materials, and equipment (Gallagher & Gallagher, 1994).

When the best interests rationale is unmasked in this way, it is hard to see gifted education as anything more than simply an additional stratum in the tracked curriculum, a super track, as I called it before, the highest and most desirable one of all. It is by no means irrelevant in this connection that advocates for gifted programs construe the *under*representation of minorities, girls, and children with disabilities as a serious problem.[10] For this worry makes sense only if, going beyond merely responding to "needs," gifted education is viewed in a positive light, so that excluding groups from it may be considered labeling them inferior. This is just the opposite of the way things work in special education. There it is the *over*representation of various groups that creates the worry.

Of course, a strong contingent of gifted-education advocates expresses skepticism about the construct of giftedness and raises serious questions about models of gifted education that rely on identification and segregation (e.g., Tannenbaum, 1991; Treffinger, 1991)—the kind of presuppositions that underlie the criticisms advanced so far. This group advocates a much more flexible and inclusive conception of giftedness and improved schooling for all children, so that a broad range of gifts can be stimulated to emerge over a relatively long period of time.

But these advocates for the gifted merely trade one set of problems for another. The more the construct of giftedness is broadened, the more the segregation of students in terms of it comes to resemble garden-variety tracking. Alternatively, the less students are segregated on the basis of their ascribed gifts, the more gifted education takes on the aspect of interest-driven curriculum differentiation, as described in the previous section. In either case, giftedness loses its value altogether as a principle for organizing schooling.

Special Education

In this section I return to my tripartite division among conceptions of equality of educational opportunity: formal, compensatory, and participatory. This framework is especially well-suited for examining special education vis-à-vis segregation.

In its purer forms, a formal interpretation of equality of educational opportunity is completely inadequate for children with disabilities. A wheelchair-bound child, for instance, will not find it very helpful that the school doors are open to everyone if the only way to the classroom is up a flight of stairs. To have any equalizing potential whatsoever, then, equality of educational opportunity requires removing physical barriers to access. This is obvious enough.

Also obvious is that merely removing physical barriers is insufficient. Consider the case of Amy Rowley, a hearing-impaired first grader, who was provided a hearing aid and training in signing and lip reading by her school. Amy's hearing impairment means that she requires additional—and different—instructional resources once she has gained physical access to the classroom, resources that mitigate her disability in order to equalize her educational opportunities.

This provides a paradigmatic case of the compensatory interpretation of equality of educational opportunity, and it is safe to say that this interpretation dominates policy and practice in special education today (though it often goes under the pejoratives of "normalization," "assimilation," and the "deficit model"). How it works with respect to special education differs little from how it works with respect to other disadvantages: In the name of equality of educational opportunity, children with disabilities are to have their disadvantages mitigated as far as possible in order to have a fair chance of attaining the educational outcomes deemed worthwhile.

In my earlier critiques of the compensatory interpretation (Chapters 2–4), I suggested that certain "disadvantaged" groups might *not want* compensation because of the cost it exacts from them in terms of their identities. This criticism may be applied to compensating for disabilities as well, and there is a complication. Not only may persons with disabilities not want compensation, but also compensation may be *fruitless*, even when persons with disabilities are willing to accept the cost that compensation can exact in terms of identities. As the lecturer-activist Norman Kunc (1992) observes, no amount of therapy will enable a child with cerebral palsy to walk or talk normally (Kunc himself has cerebral palsy). To persist with compensation under such circumstances, Kunc says, is to condemn such a child to a "life sentence" of marginalization.

How does the participatory interpretation fare in the context of special education? To answer this question, it is useful to distinguish between two general kinds of cases: those that present a realistic chance of achieving the participatory educational ideal and those that do not.

The first kind of case, exemplified by Norman Kunc as a child, is straightforward. All children who are capable of attaining the participatory educational ideal should be provided with educational effort and resources sufficient to achieve it, and different children will require different amounts.

In cases like this the participatory interpretation resembles the compensatory interpretation, and there is no inconsistency here. Compensation is not inherently objectionable; whether it is depends on who defines the needs and goals and whether they are controversial. In this connection, compensating Amy Rowley in the form of a hearing aid and training in signing and lip reading toward the goal of improved communication seems uncontroversial enough.[11] But this is different from insisting that her enunciation be perfect in order that she be normal and whole. The chief complaint against the compensatory interpretation, broadly construed, is that it takes the traditional goals and norms of schooling for granted and, compensating as deemed necessary, applies them indifferently to all children.

Adopting the participatory educational ideal as the overriding obligation of public schooling has specific implications for the practice of special education. Foremost among these is the strong support it provides for inclusion, as against segregation. Affording recognition and being recognized are reciprocal, and both are required to foster democratic character. There is no surer way of doing this than by providing face-to-face practice in deliberating with those who have different values, interests, talents, and life circumstances. Inclusion is thus a necessary condition of fostering equality of educational opportunity under its participatory interpretation.

But it is obviously not a sufficient condition. *Mere* inclusion, for instance, physically including children with disabilities in regular classrooms but otherwise excluding them from meaningful participation, can do little to promote equality of educational opportunity. Even when done well, however, inclusion still may not be sufficient. For there exists the second kind of case distinguished above, in which a child's disabilities give her or him no realistic chance of attaining the participatory ideal.

Take a child with "significantly limited intellectual capacity" (SLIC). For such a child we might adopt the goal of fostering a sense of "belonging" (Kunc, 1992) rather than promoting full-blown equality of educational opportunity. This response squares with the considerations adduced by care theorists and communitarians and also supports inclusion. I think it is basically correct, but I attach one important proviso: that it not be construed so as to reintroduce the forced choice between social justice and equality of educational opportunity, on the one hand, and caring and belonging, on the other (see Chapter 3).

When (full-blown) equality of educational opportunity cannot be achieved, as the kind of cases in question assume, social justice still makes demands, including educational ones. In this vein, the participatory interpretation has as one of its requirements that *all* persons be afforded recognition and secured self-respect, a requirement that can be met here. Rather than being goals separate from social justice, or at odds with it, fostering, caring, community, and a sense of belonging are its prerequisites. Thus an emphasis on caring, community, and a sense of belonging should not be seen as *alternative* to an emphasis on social justice.

For the sake of completeness, I now consider a variant of cases of the second type, in which, arguably at least, not only are the cognitive demands of the participatory ideal out of reach but also the sense of belonging. These are truly tragic cases, in which a child's disabilities are so severe that the capacity for meaningful human interaction seems altogether absent. Consider Tommy, a 5-year-old with such severe brain damage that his human interaction is limited to moving his head in the direction of people's voices.[12]

Cases like Tommy's require us to pay careful attention to the history of exclusion in special education and to be mindful of a ''slippery slope'' form of reasoning that fails to distinguish among the very different kinds of needs and capabilities of children with different kinds of disabilities (Howe & Miramontes, 1992). But even if one bears in mind this caveat, it is difficult to see how children like Tommy can themselves derive any benefits that are *educational* in any real sense from schooling. In turn, this makes it difficult to see how to apply the argument that social justice requires providing Tommy with his fair share of education. This is not to say that social justice is beside the point in cases like Tommy's. On the contrary, social justice requires that Tommy be cared for, both to serve his interests and the interests of his parents (who deserve the same freedom from responsibilities for day care and its costs that any other parents experience). Rather, it is to say that there is no principled reason for *schools* to provide the kind of care Tommy needs. Social justice demands they do it because (in the United States at least) no other options are available.

CONCLUSION

Equality of educational opportunity is under siege. It has been identified both as the chief culprit in ''dumbing down'' the curriculum and as the tool of arrogant, know-it-all bureaucrats. So long as the average classroom remains the kind of dismal, mind-numbing place it is (Goodlad, 1984); so long as performing well in the traditional high-track curriculum provides the ticket to expanded opportunity; and so long as inadequate funding forces difficult choices, pressures will persist to stratify the public schools in order to insure that the most talented receive a good education.

Given currently prevailing political winds, responding to pressures to promote the welfare of these children threatens to increasingly come at the expense of the welfare of less advantaged ones. Two policy proposals have emerged that are garnering increasing support: rigorous standards and testing regimens and schools of choice. Why these measures are ineffectual and worse are the topics of the next two chapters.

CHAPTER 6

Testing

For some thirteen centuries, the Chinese government recruited its officials through an intricate system of examinations. . . . The purpose of the examination system was, first, to break up the hereditary aristocracy and, second, to collect talent for the state. ''The world's men of unusual ambitions have been trapped in my bag!'' boasted the emperor T'ai-tsung (627–649) after watching a procession of new graduates.

—Michael Walzer, Spheres of Justice

The twofold purpose of testing that Walzer (1983) describes has a quite modern ring. Just as testing was justified in the ancient Chinese civil service system, testing is commonly advanced today as both a fair means of distributing opportunities—because it rewards talent rather than birthright—and an efficient means—because it puts talent in service to society. One of the major problems that beset the Chinese system also has a modern ring: Individuals who were talented but disadvantaged by social circumstances did not perform well on the examinations. Thus insuring equality of educational opportunity was required for testing to achieve its purposes. According to Walzer, this is something it never managed to do.

Despite the caution the Chinese experience should encourage, testing has become a central mechanism in the United States for distributing opportunities. Testing is now an industry in the full sense of the word—complete with large corporations—and testing for the purpose of awarding employment opportunities has been extended well beyond civil service to include employment of tremendous variety, ranging from barbering to medicine. In education, testing has for some time served the various roles of diagnosis, selection, and accountability. More recently, it has come to occupy a central role in proposals for school reform. It is variously touted as the key to improving student and teacher performance, the curriculum, and economic competitiveness. More than ever, it seems, educational testing is viewed as a magic elixir for curing education's ills.

A magic elixir educational testing most assuredly is not. As in the Chinese experience, inequality of educational opportunity poses a significant obstacle to claims made for testing systems, particularly when promoting equality is added to the list. Ample research evidence shows that educational testing works to disadvantage various minority groups as well as girls and women (AAUW, 1991; Gould, 1981; Haney, 1984, 1993; Oakes, 1985, 1990). As a consequence, educational testing schemes often do much more to rationalize inequality than they do to mitigate it.

But the argument of this chapter is getting ahead of itself. That certain groups are ''disadvantaged'' by educational testing, in the sense that they receive different opportunities as a result of it, provides only a prima facie case that educational testing promotes an objectionable form of inequality. There may be ways of justifying the decisions made on the basis of differential test performance that are consistent with the requirements of equality. This chapter critically examines this general proposition, particularly the claims for testing incorporated into educational reform proposals over approximately the last 10 years.

The argument has two basic strands. In the first, I briefly describe *consequentialist* conceptions of test validity (Messick, 1989; Shepard, 1993). In contrast to those who may be termed *technicists*, who abstract questions of test validity and test bias from social conditions, consequentialist theorists deny a sharp distinction between science and values. They see questions of test validity and bias as unavoidably embedded in social conditions and, accordingly, hold that testing practices must be evaluated in terms of the broad social consequences that result from their use. Consequentialist theorists thus open the door that separates questions of test validity and bias from questions of social justice.

But opening this door is only an initial step, for it leaves undetermined precisely what social arrangements and consequences are just and how testing should be evaluated in terms of these. In the second strand of my argument, I take the consequentialist perspective as my point of departure and then investigate how educational testing practices ought to be circumscribed by the demands of justice, particularly the requirement of equality of educational opportunity. I explicate and evaluate reform proposals from *A Nation at Risk* (1983) through *Goals 2000* (1994a) in terms of the three conceptions of equality of educational opportunity I have employed throughout.

VALIDITY, BIAS, AND JUSTICE IN EDUCATIONAL TESTING: THE LIMITS OF THE CONSEQUENTIALIST CONCEPTION

Educational measurement has been historically dominated by technicists. Technicists abstract questions of test validity and bias from social conditions and maintain that everyone should play by the ground rules that they, the technical experts, set. This requires, first, defining the primary problem as obtaining accurate measurements and, second, embracing a sharp distinction between scientific investigation and value judgments. When the game is played by these rules, investigating the validity of testing is put squarely in the category of scientific investigation and is thereby insulated from broader questions about social justice.

Recently, consequentialists have come to the fore in educational measurement. Consequentialists deny the sharp distinction between scientific investigation and value judgments embraced by technicists and see questions of test validity and bias as unavoidably embedded in social conditions. Accordingly, they hold that educational testing practices must be evaluated in terms of the broad social consequences that result from their use.

Whatever its advantages over the technicist conception (some of which I discuss as my arguments unfold), the consequentialist conception contains a crucial ambiguity regarding the relationship between test validity and social justice. In particular, it is open to a strong (or categorical) interpretation and a weak (or hypothetical) interpretation. Given a strong interpretation, value judgments are internal to validity, such that "X use of testing is valid" entails "X use of testing ought to be employed." Given a weak interpretation, value judgments are external to validity, such that "X use of testing is valid" entails "X use of testing ought to be employed *given* value commitment Y."

In this section I argue that because a consequentialist conception is committed to the weak interpretation, it does not distance itself as much from a technicist conception as its advocates seem to believe. In a bit of a digression, I also make a few observations about the putative promise of performance assessment (the latest measurement fetish) to foster equality of educational opportunity.

Some Observations About Validity and Bias

Whatever one's position on educational testing, the elimination of bias is a minimal requirement of its just use. Questions of test bias are closely related to questions of test validity. A test (test use) is valid if it measures what it purports to and invalid if it does not. Bias is a kind of invalidity that arises relative to groups. In general, a test is biased against a particular group if it underpredicts their performance on the criterion of interest relative to some other group(s). Charges of bias typically arise when a given identifiable group scores low on a test relative to some other group(s).[1] For example, the SAT is charged with bias against women on the grounds that although women generally score lower than men, their scores correlate with higher college performance (AAUW, 1991).

The kind of bias just described is conventionally termed *predictive*. (Later I distinguish this variety of bias from *criterion* bias.) Historically, two conceptions of predictive bias have predominated: "external" and "internal" (Camilli & Shepard, 1994). External conceptions construe the problem of bias in terms of how well a test predicts the real-world performance it is designed to measure. (The above example of college entrance examinations and women provides an illustration of this conception.) Internal conceptions construe the problem of bias in terms of characteristics internal to the test, particularly differences among items. For example, suppose a mathematics achievement test contains an item that makes use of knowledge about the layout of a football field and that women score poorly on this item both relative to men and relative to their overall performance on the test. If so, the item is biased. If, on the other hand, women score low on this item relative to men but not relative to their overall performance on the test (which entails that they score lower overall than men), the item is not biased.

The proposal that justice may be achieved by employing internally unbiased tests may be dismissed as just so much technical hocus-pocus. Put simply, rendering tests internally unbiased fails to insure that performance of interest is being measured or can be accurately predicted. To take the previous example of college entrance examinations, it is altogether possible that women could consistently score low relative to men such that no particular item correlated poorly with the remainder of items. Given an internal conception, the examination is not biased against women. But it is quite sensible to ask whether the examination as a whole is biased against women relative to some relevant external criterion of performance, for example, college grades. If women did achieve grades at least as high as men [and they in fact do (AAUW, 1991)], then, provided grades are an appropriate criterion of college performance, the examination would be clearly biased against women and would, accordingly, be an unjust means of making admissions decisions. This general problem with internal conceptions leads some measurement experts to conclude (e.g., Camilli & Shepard, 1994) that internal bias analyses should be limited to serving as flags for use in test development and, in particular, should never supplant external analyses.

The proposal that justice may be achieved by eliminating external bias is considerably more defensible than the proposal that it may be achieved by eliminating internal bias. For, unlike internally unbiased tests, which provide no guarantee of being appropriately related to performance criteria, externally unbiased tests are so related by definition.

But achieving a strong relationship between test performance and performance on external criteria is also insufficient to insure justice. In addition to the kind of predictive bias I've described so far, tests may also encounter the problem of criterion bias. In contrast to the question of predictive bias, which is whether group members' promise is accurately assessed *given* some criterion of performance, the question of criterion bias is whether the criterion of performance is itself biased against groups, independent of how well it correlates with test scores.

Criterion bias may take two forms: across and within. Across-criteria bias occurs when test performance is too heavily emphasized relative to other qualifications. Overreliance on testing inflates the importance of criteria that it can accurately measure—various academic talents and accomplishments, in particular—to the point of viewing these criteria as all-purpose qualifications that should be negotiable currency in virtually any arena. In general, qualifications cannot be viewed apart from the scheme of social cooperation from which they gain their meaning. For example, if we assume that more women should be in positions of authority in elementary education in order to help eliminate the sexist attitudes produced by the present disproportionate number of men who occupy these positions, women then have a qualification that men lack for admission to graduate programs in educational administration and ultimately for appointment to administrative posts (Gutmann, 1987). If we assume that minorities should be admitted to universities in order to help overcome racism and stereotyping, and to make available to university communities a diversity of life experiences and perspectives, then they have a qualification that nonminorities lack. The failure to appreciate the full spectrum of qualifications associated with a given educational or employment opportunity often fuels the complaint that it is unjust to prefer women over men and minorities over nonminorities when the latter are ''more qualified'' (read: score higher on tests). The problem is exacerbated when positions become more scarce, for the solution is often the convenient (and mindless) one of simply ''raising standards'' (for example, raising the cut scores on college admissions tests used to determine which applicants will be given further consideration).

Within-criterion bias is bias in its most insidious form. Performance criteria may be perfectly matched and appropriately weighed relative to a given domain of performance, yet still be defined so that advantages and disadvantages arise associated with various characteristics such as race, social class, and gender. To take a fanciful example, imagine a test for Grand Wizard of the KKK (the Grand Wizard test, or GWT). The GWT could be unbiased in the sense of being a perfectly accurate predictor of poor on-the-job performance by African Americans. Of course, it is the performance itself, carrying out the duties of the Grand Wizard, that renders the GWT biased against African Americans. To take a more realistic example, if the curricula and pedagogy of the U.S. educational system are indeed heavily biased in favor of White males (a charge leveled frequently), then criteria of performance are ipso facto biased in favor of White males as well. Under these kinds of conditions, eliminating predictive bias from educational tests can do little to eliminate injustice. All it can do is improve predictions of who will perform well given the criteria of performance associated with those who have historically enjoyed advantages within unjust institutional arrangements.

The Consequentialist Conception of Validity

Proponents of a consequentialist theory of test validity embrace a much more expansive conception that avoids many of the problems that plague the technicist conception. Consequentialist theorists object to relying on a single correlation as evidence for validity, a practice that remains pervasive (Shepard, 1993), requiring instead multiple sources of evidence. In their view, both the intended uses of tests and their associated social consequences must be included in the evaluation of a test's validity (Messick, 1989; Shepard, 1993).

Shepard (1993), for instance, suggestively likens the difference between technicist and consequentialist conceptions of validity to the difference between settling for "truth in labeling" and demanding that testing be also "safe and effective." As an illustration, she appeals to the practice of readiness testing. According to her, the validity of readiness testing cannot be established solely on the basis of its ability to predict who will do well or poorly. Rather, to be valid ("safe and effective"), its use should not serve to "hurt" students to whom it is applied, especially those who are deemed not ready for given educational experiences. This requires investigating the broad range of consequences that attend the use of readiness testing.

Consequentialist theorists thus dismiss the technicist notion that the evaluation of educational testing can be divorced from social conse-quences and implicit value commitments. So far, so good. Having come to this point, however, they demur, leaving open the question of pre-cisely what criteria are to be used to determine when educational testing is just. As a result, or so I argue, the technicist science/values distinction remains a central presupposition.

Shepard (1993), who provides a history of the emerging dominance of the consequentialist perspective in the measurement community and who wholeheartedly endorses this development, provides a case in point.

> [V]alidity investigations cannot resolve questions that are purely value choices (e.g., should students be given an academic curriculum versus being tracked into vocational and college preparation programs?). How-ever, to the extent that contending constituencies make competing claims about what a test measures, about the nature of its relations to subsequent performance in school or on the job, or about the effects of testing, these value-laden questions are integral to a validity evaluation. For example, the question as to whether students are helped or hurt as a result of test-based remedial placement is amenable to scientific investigation. (p. 429)

It would seem that Shepard owes us a further explanation of what decisions are to count as "purely value choices." Take the ques-tion of tracking students into vocational education, and consider the following empirical questions that are pertinent to answering it. Can tests accurately predict who should be in which track? Do those in the vocational track wind up with jobs? Are their jobs satisfying? Do they receive adequate salaries in these jobs? Do they forgo aspects of the curriculum relevant to effective citizenship? And so forth. Presumably, and as she herself indeed suggests, she would want to include these and similar questions in evaluating testing for the purposes of placement in vocational education. But, then, how does the original question about tracking involve "purely value choices"?

Shepard's (1993) subsequent example of test-based remedial place-ment does little to clarify matters. On the contrary, it is supposed to be an example of a value-laden question that *is* amenable to scientific investigation. But it is difficult to see how it is any different from the "purely" value-laden issue of tracking. Indeed, there is no way to eval-uate test-based remedial placement adequately without addressing the questions of what it is to "hurt" a student and when this might indeed be justified, questions that cannot be disentangled from (purely value-laden?) others like what is fair to other students? what builds character?

when must students suffer deserved consequences? what practices are most cost-effective?

Shepard's (1993) difficulty in breaking with the technicist way of thinking is linked to the question of social justice more directly in her discussion of using a multiple-criteria approach for admission to selective colleges. She defends the use of the SAT as an adjunct to other criteria, such as music or athletic talent, minority group status, and geographical distribution:

> At one level, examination of these selection practices might provoke a debate between different philosophical positions. Should decisions be guided by meritocratic or other theories of social justice. . . . At a more technical level, [multiple criteria] can be defended "scientifically" given that academic predictors are both incomplete and fallible predictors of success. . . . Therefore, [the] value perspective [associated with multiple criteria] holds that colleges can reasonably select among qualified applicants using criteria aimed at other goals such as increasing the diversity of perspectives represented among their students. This value choice cannot be resolved within the validity framework but should be made explicit and examined for consequences as part of the validity investigation. (p. 435)

Here, Shepard is concerned with avoiding what I referred to earlier as across-criteria bias, but the passage is relevant to both forms of criterion bias, and it may be used to illustrate the limitations of Shepard's (1993) consequentialist theory in addressing them. Regarding across-criteria bias, Shepard holds that criteria other than test scores may be "reasonably" employed. However, in the absence of some more substantive value commitment (e.g., increasing diversity), there is no way to determine whether, more than just being "reasonable," the criterion of race indeed ought to be included in selection decisions. Regarding within-criterion bias, in the absence of some more substantive value commitment (e.g., to recognizing diverse cultural voices within the curriculum), there is no way to determine whether the criteria of success are indeed biased against certain groups. It seems that we can eliminate neither form of criterion bias by relying solely on Shepard's "validity framework."

The Red Herring of Performance Assessment

Although not strictly within the logical flow of the argument to this point, performance assessment is well worth a slight digression. Two major claims are made on its behalf: (a) It will improve curricula and instruction, and (b) it will foster greater equity in educational testing.

Improvement in curricula and instruction will allegedly follow as a result of exploiting the practice of teaching to the test. The reasoning is roughly as follows: Teaching to the test is a given—"You get what you assess." "You do not get what you do not assess" (Resnick & Resnick, 1992, p. 59). Thus rendering the performance required on tests as close as possible to the actual performance desired will automatically drive curricula and instruction in the right directions. I do not criticize this defense of performance assessment in any detail here, since it is tangential to questions of validity and bias. I simply observe that when uniform standards and assessments are imposed top-down, by the measurement experts, they smack of coercion and betray a condescending attitude toward teachers. They are a circuitous way of addressing the shortcomings of curricula and instruction that encourages the assessment tail to continue to wag the instructional dog.[2]

The second claim for performance assessment—that it fosters greater equity—is my primary interest here. It is with respect to this claim that performance assessment is most clearly a red herring.

That performance assessment is potentially more predictively valid than traditional measures is unassailable. Having people run a 100-meter race is certainly a better way to determine their sprinting ability than having them take a multiple-choice test on the principles of running. And having students write essays is certainly a better way to determine their writing ability than giving them a multiple-choice test on the principles of writing. But suppose, having developed such performance assessments to our satisfaction, we now have to weight them to determine which applicants to State U should be admitted. The problem is that no matter how predictively valid these assessments are individually, they provide no help with the weighting problem, the problem of across-criteria bias, for this requires a judgment of the relative value of each kind of performance. For a very similar reason, performance assessment also fails to provide any help in eliminating within-criterion bias. If the desired performance is itself biased against certain groups, then having more direct measures of it is beside the point (compare a multiple-choice version of the Grand Wizard Test with a portfolio version). Worse, the patterns of differential performance among groups may well persist or increase (Apple, 1993a; Garcia & Pearson, 1994; Madaus, 1994). Performance assessment may thus exacerbate the problem of injustice by further hiding it behind a layer of the latest brand of technical veneer[3] and by providing new ammunition for those who would "blame the victim."

In the end, performance assessment provides no help whatsoever with the problem of criterion bias, and the consequentialist view winds up being simply a more sophisticated version of the technicist view—a difference of degree, not kind. Although the issue of what constitutes an acceptable "scientific" evaluation is clearly more complex in the consequentialist view, it is nonetheless conceived in a way that renders the scientific question of what uses of testing are valid contingent on "value choices." In this way, the claim that "X use of testing is valid" is always a disguised hypothetical—always of the form "X use of testing is valid *given* you endorse Y" (where Y is some value commitment, e.g., meritocracy, utilitarianism, Rawlsianism, and so forth). So long as validity judgments are construed as hypothetical, they remain incapable of determining the answer to the pressing practical question of which among competing testing schemes ought to be endorsed and put into practice. For this reason, the consequentialist conception retains the technicist's fundamental bifurcation between test validity and judgments of value. It retains the "truth in labeling" criterion as well.

If validity findings are to justify testing practices by themselves, they ultimately must be categorical, must be of the form "X use of educational testing is valid, period."[4] A categorical conception of test validity would incorporate substantive value commitments into the very meaning of "validity," and such a conception has the advantages of directing validity research in morally defensible directions and preventing measurement experts from hiding their implicit value commitments behind a cloak of scientific objectivity.[5]

TESTING, STANDARDS, AND EQUALITY OF EDUCATIONAL OPPORTUNITY

Regardless of whether value judgments are internal to a validity framework (as in the case of a categorical conception) or external to it (as in the case of a hypothetical conception), justifying a given use of testing requires embracing some underlying conception of social justice and some associated conception of equality of educational opportunity. As it turns out, advocates of testing rarely (if ever) announce the conceptions they presuppose, and they often mix conceptions. Thus here I unearth the conceptions implicit in prominent standard/test-based government education reform proposals, employing my familiar tripartite scheme.

The Formal Interpretation

Recently, testing schemes that embrace a formal interpretation of equality of educational opportunity typically have educational reform as their central aim. *A Nation at Risk* (1983) and *America 2000* (1991) are good examples. Rigorous standards and assessment (*assessment* has displaced *testing* in the vernacular and virtually goes hand-in-glove with standards[6]) are touted as the major vehicle through which reform should occur. These proposals employ a rudimentary carrot-and-stick psychology, in which students and educators alike receive presidential awards for excellence or are bludgeoned with "accountability." The basic idea is that educational results will improve if the distributions of goods such as salary, promotions, placement in advanced courses, high school diplomas, and admission to college are based on performance on rigorous assessments, which are, in turn, based on rigorous standards.

At the level of social justice one finds a confused and confusing mix of free-market libertarianism and meritocracy exemplified in formalist frameworks. For example, promoting testing to facilitate choice schemes (on the model of an educational *Consumers Report)* is rooted in free-market libertarianism, whereas promoting testing as a device for bureaucratic control based on specified performance is rooted in meritocracy. (Both these purposes are advanced in *America 2000*, for instance.)

As it turns out, the theoretical incoherence of mixing libertarian and meritocratic principles need not be belabored,[7] for educational testing schemes based on a formalist framework may be summarily dismissed on the grounds that they fail to take into account inequalities experienced by children both in and out of schools—a fact that hardly needs documentation. Because of such inequalities, children do not enjoy anything even remotely approximating equality of educational opportunity, except in some very formal and abstract sense that ignores the interaction between schooling and what children bring to it [not to mention the inequality of resources among schools themselves (Kozol, 1991)]. Thus it can hardly be just to ignore these inequalities and evaluate all students in terms of the same assessments when many of them have had little or no opportunity to master the knowledge and skills upon which such assessments are based.

This intuition about justice is no doubt responsible for the inclusion of notions such as "opportunity to learn" and "delivery standards" in more recent education reform proposals. I return to these notions shortly, after digressing to examine the kind of formalist response they have prompted.

Albert Shanker provides one such response: "We don't abolish medical school exams because not everyone has had the opportunity for top-notch pre-med education. Nor do we say that tests for airplane pilots shouldn't count because not everyone has the opportunity to do well on them" (in Leo, 1993, p. 3c). There are two ready rejoinders to Shanker's analogies. First, general educational standards—those associated with receiving a high school diploma, for example, or with the participatory educational ideal—are much more ambiguous than those associated with being a medical doctor or an airplane pilot. Furthermore, unlike the examples Shanker chooses (all too convenient for his purposes), standards for a high school diploma are ones that (nearly) everyone should meet if K–12 education is to fulfill its obligation to produce citizens who are capable of leading happy and fruitful lives and of participating in democratic decision making, whatever their occupation. Second, even in his own examples, Shanker is far too sanguine about unequal opportunities. Although not everyone can become a medical doctor, the opportunity to do so should not be heavily or exclusively determined by social circumstances that are beyond one's control.

Rather than retreating into what we *in fact do*, and begging the question in favor of the status quo, what we *ought to do* is take general measures to insure that individuals' educational opportunities are as far as possible equalized. Contra Shanker, we should avoid using "the way things happen to be" as "an excuse for ignoring injustice" (Rawls, 1971, p. 102).

The Compensatory Interpretation

Influential documents that succeeded *A Nation at Risk* (1983) and *America 2000* (1991) in the early 1990s, such as the *NCEST Report* (1992), *Goals 2000* (1994a), and the CRESST conference on equity (Rothman, 1994), each assume a compensatory interpretation of equality of educational opportunity.[8] Specifically, because these proposals incorporate equalizing "delivery standards" (conditions of schooling) to insure that students receive an equal "opportunity to learn," they incorporate the intuition that it is unjust to hold students who have not had adequate educational opportunities responsible for achieving the same level of educational performance as students who have. They also hold that such inequality of educational opportunity should be mitigated.

To complicate matters, "delivery standards" and "opportunities to learn" may be interpreted in terms of either of the two kinds of more comprehensive compensatory frameworks introduced in Chapter 2: utilitarian and liberal-egalitarian.

THE UTILITARIAN FRAMEWORK. The utilitarian justification for standards and testing is strongly economic. The basic idea is that by applying rigorous standards and assessments to all students, and by developing the talents of individuals who are disadvantaged in the name of equal educational opportunity, the economic health and leadership of the United States will be restored.

This kind of reasoning exemplifies what Nel Noddings (1992) calls the "ideology of control." The impulse for control runs deep in U.S. education, spurred and reinforced by positivist social science and the associated technocratic solutions to political and educational problems it encourages (Howe, 1992). This impulse has been heavily fueled in the last decade by the attempt to lay the blame for a faltering economy and other social difficulties at the doorstep of education, and it involves a pronounced and explicit appeal to competition. (Consider the ludicrous sports-inspired notion of "world-class standards," introduced in 1991 in *America 2000* and now part of the vernacular.) As it turns out, the supposed relationship between the nation's economic health and its levels of educational achievement, presupposed in much of the rhetoric, is quite weak (Bracey, 1992; House, 1991; Spring, 1984). And this serves to undermine a utilitarian framework.

Furthermore, as observed in Chapter 2, a utilitarian framework renders the commitment to equality of educational opportunity precarious. That is, equality of opportunity could be (is) suspended in order to achieve the overarching aim of maximizing benefit. Because the shape of the distribution of benefits, including the gap between the most and least advantaged, does not enter into utilitarian calculations, utilitarian-based testing schemes sanction distributing educational resources away from the most marginalized and poverty-stricken individuals in society toward those most likely to make good engineers and scientists, typically the already advantaged. This smacks of injustice in no small way.

THE LIBERAL-EGALITARIAN FRAMEWORK. A liberal-egalitarian framework recognizes that individuals come by their talents in ways that are largely beyond their control—as if by the luck of the draw (Rawls, 1971). One cannot choose one's parents, talents, or physical condition. This renders natural talents "arbitrary from a moral point of view," which is to say that individuals deserve neither credit nor blame for the natural talents they possess or fail to possess, for the social circumstances into which they are born, or for what flows from either of these factors. In turn, insofar as distributing society's goods and opportunities on the basis of merit assumes that individuals do indeed deserve to be rewarded for their talents and social circumstances, such a principle of merit must be rejected as unjust.

This is not to suggest that it is inherently unjust to distribute goods and opportunities on the basis of talents, particularly acquired ones.

The justificatory principle, however, is "legitimate expectations" rather than just desserts (Rawls, 1971). That is, although individuals do not deserve their station in life, strictly speaking, they nevertheless form expectations against a background of social practices and institutions.[9] There are circumstances under which such expectations ought to be satisfied for individuals who live up to the demands associated with them, namely, when the social practices and institutions in which the system of expectations and rewards is embedded are just.

One of the central requirements for just background conditions is what Rawls (1971) calls *fair* equality of opportunity, a concept akin to the notion of opportunities worth wanting and one that can be naturally extended to include fair equality of *educational* opportunity. Fair equality of educational opportunity requires going beyond formal equality of opportunity and intervening in order to mitigate contingencies that disadvantage individuals through no fault of their own, such as being born with a handicap or into poverty. In addition to being antimeritocratic, fair equality of educational opportunity is also anti-utilitarian. It construes equality of educational opportunity as fundamental, such that it serves as a check on what is done in the name of maximizing benefit.

Insofar as current reform proposals detach the justification for "delivery standards" and "opportunities to learn" from utilitarian justifications, they may well incorporate the idea of fair equality of educational opportunity. But even so, they fall considerably short of what liberal-egalitarianism requires in the name of justice. Because fair equality of educational opportunity focuses exclusively on mitigating disadvantages in the interests of rendering competition fair, the principle is too narrow to stand alone. For example, suppose that we do all we can to mitigate the educational disadvantages experienced by a child with significant brain damage. Are we then justified in letting the chips fall where they may, having done all we can to render the competition fair? Obviously not. In general, fair equality of educational opportunity is consistent with vastly unequal capabilities which, despite our best efforts, can lead to vastly unequal results that are unacceptable from the perspective of justice. Thus fair equality of opportunity cannot by itself determine how to distribute opportunities and benefits justly. It must be augmented with an egalitarian (and explicitly nonutilitarian) principle of distribution (e.g., the kind of threshold principle I defended in Chapter 2). Given such a principle, utilitarian trade-offs of the kind described previously, in which the educationally less advantaged must sacrifice in a way that benefits the educationally more advantaged, are precluded in yet another way.

Liberal-egalitarianism may take (and often has taken) compensatory forms. And where it does, it may be charged with what by this point should be a familiar criticism: Compensatory frameworks uncritically assume a universal ideal of education that embodies the historical dominance of White males. In the context of the standards/testing rhetoric, the point is that a plan for compensating children, readying them, and providing them with opportunities to learn is misguided and ineffective if the ideal in terms of which they are compensated, readied, and provided opportunities to learn is irrelevant or threatening.

It is a short step from here to a sweeping criticism of the approach to standards and assessment that dominates today. The traditional liberal arts curriculum has been echoed in government reports since *A Nation at Risk* (1983), and the emphasis on x level of performance in traditional liberal arts subjects (particularly math and science) continues unabated. It is thus difficult to regard the present clarion call for more precise and rigorous educational standards and assessments as doing anything other than simply articulating and further entrenching the educational status quo (Apple, 1993b; Martin, 1994, chap. 12). And, as noted earlier in this chapter, the status quo has not been particularly congenial to marginalized groups. Assessing all children in terms of it is thus open to the charge of criterion bias—bias implicit in the very standards that are to serve as the anchor of valid assessment. If educational standards and assessments were based on uncontested educational practices and ideals, then within-criterion bias would not be a problem and a compensatory framework (at least in its liberal-egalitarian form) would have much to recommend it. But because educational practices and ideals are not uncontested, they need to be negotiated, or *re*negotiated, as the case may be. This leads me once again to the participatory educational ideal.

The Participatory Interpretation

However intertwined and permeable the boundaries, a participatory framework can be thought of as having two levels: the political and the personal. In Chapter 3, I argued that, initial appearances notwithstanding, these two levels can be rendered consistent. Here I presuppose that analysis and apply it to standards and assessment. The political level is identified with the fundamental educational aim of fostering democratic character. The personal level is identified with the fundamental educational aim of fostering a secure sense of self-worth (valuable in its own right and also conducive to democratic participation). The question I address is how to formulate educational standard setting and assessment so as to further these two aims. I begin with the political level.

THE POLITICAL LEVEL. When democratic character is made the locus of educational standard setting (rather than economic efficiency or reverence for the liberal arts, for instance), questions about whether to teach math, science, literature, social studies, and so forth, how much of these subjects should be taught, and to whom, must be viewed in a different light. Take the science curriculum. Questions concerning it tend to be put in the abstract. The general question of how much and what kind of science needs to be taught leads to questions such as, Is knowledge of photosynthesis required? mastery of the periodic table? skills in tree identification? familiarity with Newton's second law? The question begging to be asked is, Required for what?

Adopting the goal of fostering democratic character doesn't make these questions any easier to answer. Instead, it suggests why asking them in the way depicted above is misguided. The goal of democratic character requires fostering general habits of mind that render individuals capable of and disposed to gathering and evaluating information, scientific and otherwise. There is little in the way of "content knowledge" that everyone needs to know (which is not to say that everyone needs to know only a little). As Jane Roland Martin (1994) observes, decisions have to be made about what to include in and exclude from the curriculum. To believe that traditional "domains of knowledge" are worthwhile a priori is to commit what Martin (chap. 9) calls the "epistemological fallacy" and to submerge historical biases. Although all students need to learn to think like democratic citizens, it is by no means obvious that they all need to learn to think like scientists, mathematicians, historians, literary critics, and philosophers. Indeed, how could they master all of these perspectives?

The kinds of "content standards" currently touted emphasize "core" academic goals—in English, history and geography, and especially mathematics and science—and crowd out the political goal of fostering democratic character. They install traditional educational goals as the be-all and end-all of public education as well as the means of distributing virtually all educational opportunities. Citizenship gets little more than lip service; notably, it is not a "core" subject and no performance standards whatsoever (let alone the "world-class" variety) attach to it.

The alternative standard of democratic character is likely to be criticized from certain quarters on the grounds that because it is amorphous as well as open-ended, it is both difficult to capture in terms of rigorous standards and a poor candidate for precise measurement. But to reject it for this reason places the quest for accurate measurement—and control—above the quest for educationally and politically defensible policies.

THE PERSONAL LEVEL. U.S. public education is indeed in serious trouble. The major problem, however, is not the absence of accountability and uniformly high standards and expectations but the system's failure to respond to the inequality wrought by the vast diversity of talents, interests, and needs. Any curriculum should include basic and pervasive educational aims such as literacy, rudimentary computation skills, and traditional subject matter, including science, mathematics, and literature. But it should also permit—and encourage—students to pursue certain of these areas in depth to the exclusion of others. Noddings (1992) is right to claim that subjecting all children to the same curriculum and standards throughout their K–12 experience guarantees that outcomes will be unequal and that many of them will fail.

The pedagogy that complements such a curriculum entails much closer relationships and much greater give-and-take among teachers and students than now characterizes public education. Fostering healthy relationships between educators and students, for students' current as well as future well-being, requires taking students' interests, aspirations, talents, and foibles seriously in order to cement their sense of self-worth and enable them to relate effectively to others. This, in turn, requires a significant level of participation on their part, in both negotiating and pursuing educational aims and activities. It also counts heavily against uniform standards and assessments. Consistent with rejecting the "ideology of control" and a truncated set of educational objectives, an open-ended form of assessment, including self-assessment, should be the norm. And it should be anchored in the diverse accomplishments of which children are capable rather than in a rigid set of preestablished goals and standards. As Noddings (1992) says, "[W]e should move away from the question, Has Johnny learned X? to the far more pertinent question, What has Johnny learned?" (p. 179).

Notwithstanding what the general tenor of my arguments might suggest, I should make clear that a participatory framework does not entail a wholesale rejection of educational assessment. It does not condemn locally designed assessments that have primarily a formative purpose,[10] and it does not condemn large-scale testing for the purposes of monitoring educational outcomes, on the model of NAEP. Nor does it even condemn a system of educational assessment used for distributing educational opportunities, at least when used relatively late in students' educational careers. It condemns educational assessment only when it is practiced in a way that is blind to the requirements of equality of educational opportunity.

Were these requirements kept in view, the need to compete for worthwhile educational opportunities would be greatly reduced. When competition for such educational opportunities did arise—say, for positions in highly selective universities—we would be in a much better position than we are now to say that the competition is just.

CONCLUSION

Goals 2000: The Educate America Act was enacted into law on March 31, 1994. Shortly after, at the annual convention of the American Educational Research Association, much interest and some optimism, coupled with a good deal of uncertainty, were evinced about what "opportunity to learn" standards would bring. One proffered interpretation equated "opportunity to learn" with the "value added" by education.[11] This kind of economics lingo is indicative of the mind-set that continues to hold sway. Moreover, the conception it embodies is indistinguishable from one of the outcomes-based definitions of equality of educational opportunity James Coleman (1968) entertained and rejected nearly 30 years ago. Such a conception requires only that schooling prevent the relative disadvantages experienced by certain groups upon entering school from becoming worse upon their exit; it does not require that results be equalized. And the "value added" interpretation is progressive by comparison with the interpretation of "opportunity to learn" then emanating from the Congress and the Department of Education.[12]

Present priorities are so egregiously—I should say savagely—misaligned that even a compensatory framework seems completely out of reach, at least in its more egalitarian forms. It strains credulity and belies even a modest commitment to equality of educational opportunity to suggest that implementing national standards and assessments could be anywhere near as effective a means of improving educational opportunity as addressing the conditions of schooling directly. It is rather like suggesting that the way to end world hunger is first to develop more rigorous standards of nutrition and then to provide physicians with more precise means of measuring ratios of muscle to fat.

CHAPTER 7

School Choice

> *It does not require an extended philosophical analysis to say something significant about how schooling should not be distributed: not by the market—children of poor and uninterested parents will not receive it; not by unconstrained democratic decision—children of disfavored minorities will be relegated to inferior schools. This much should be common-sensically clear and is broadly acknowledged in the United States, at least today.*
>
> *—Amy Gutmann,* Democratic Education

Some 10 years after its writing, in the wake of burgeoning support for "schools of choice," Gutmann's (1987) claims seem overconfident at best, flat wrong at worst. But her mistake is simply failing to anticipate the wide support schools of choice would garner and, accordingly, underestimating how much counterargument is required. Otherwise, her general thesis—that schools of choice are largely inconsistent with both equality of educational opportunity and democracy—is sound. This chapter elaborates this thesis.

That school choice schemes come in a variety of forms associated with a variety of justifications significantly complicates this undertaking. I begin with the two rationales for choice singled out by Gutmann: strong parental autonomy and the market. I find good reasons for rejecting each. I then take up what I call the communitarian rationale. I find this rationale more defensible than the first two but nonetheless seriously flawed because it ignores the trade-offs that have to be made to insure equality. Finally, I take up the pragmatic rationale. Under this rationale, I find some place for expanded choice, provided it is sufficiently circumscribed.

THE STRONG PARENTAL AUTONOMY RATIONALE

Various school choice advocates who rest their case on strong parental autonomy share the view that education, especially moral-political education, is a private matter that should be left to parental discretion. The appeal to strong parental autonomy makes for some strange bedfellows among school choice advocates. At one end of the spectrum are libertarians, for whom school choice serves to foster liberty. At the other end are moral conservatives, for whom school choice serves to foster correct beliefs and dispositions in their children and to insulate them from the corrupting influences of modern society. Whereas libertarians embrace school choice as a matter of principle, moral conservatives embrace it as a matter of strategy. Thus, whereas libertarians condemn uniform, compulsory schooling per se, moral conservatives condemn it only insofar as it fails to promote what is in their eyes the morally best way of life.

As I argued in Chapter 2, libertarianism may be convincingly criticized for making much too little of how the context of choice determines the worth of the educational opportunities available to various children. This criticism applies with particular force to school choice schemes. Thoroughgoing libertarians—those opposed to compulsory public education in any form[1]—permit not just wide disparities in determining the worth of educational opportunities. Because parents are the sole authority on what school a child should attend (if any), educational opportunities may be withheld altogether. This follows because the public is precluded not only from making any claims on behalf of its own interests in promoting a productive democratic citizenry but also from making any claims on behalf of the interests of children.

It is difficult to take such an extreme view seriously. Consistently applied, it would require abolishing not only public schooling but also child labor laws, laws prohibiting child abuse and neglect, and virtually any intervention by the public to promote the welfare of children. From the point of view of the public, the libertarian proposal leaves the prospect of a democratic and productive citizenry wholly to chance. From the point of view of children, the libertarian proposal gives parents unconstrained control over their children's welfare. It renders children totally at the mercy of their parents' resources and motivation, providing certain of them with only the barest kinds of educational opportunities and others with significant advantages.

Libertarians must thus moderate their opposition to the public's right to limit parental autonomy in the name of children's health, safety, and intellectual development, and contemporary libertarian commentators do just that (e.g., Kane, 1992). But this serves to dilute their view significantly, for it changes the question from *whether* the public has a legitimate role in promoting equality of educational opportunity to *how great* the public's role should be. School choice, in turn, must be evaluated in these relative terms.

Although moral conservatives join libertarians in championing strong parental autonomy, as I observed before, they do so on the basis of strategy rather than principle. They are thus open to the charge that they are inconsistent, that they want to have it both ways. I have in mind especially the radical religious right, which is simultaneously working on two ostensibly incompatible fronts. First, it is engaged in well-known activities to influence the public schools by spearheading efforts to ban books, eliminate sex education, and reintroduce school prayer.[2] These efforts are grounded in uniform public schooling for all children, at the expense of parental autonomy. Second, it is also at the forefront of home schooling and is actively engaged in establishing its own academies and charter schools. These efforts are grounded in parental autonomy, at the expense of uniform public schooling.

So long as activities of the second kind—promoting school choice—are seen as parts of the stratagem for achieving the aims of those of the first kind—transforming the education of all children—these activities are not inconsistent. But the inconsistency is removed only by making parental autonomy secondary to achieving the right kind of uniform public schooling and by adopting schools of choice as an ad hoc response to a kind of public schooling that the religious right sees as hostile to its particular vision of the good and moral life.

In my view, the moral conservatives' position is more defensible than the libertarians', precisely because it does not rest on unconstrained parental autonomy. But this renders moral conservatives indistinguishable in their general position from other groups who see school choice as the vehicle through which they can avoid the perceived oppressive effects of present public schools on their children. Of course, just what constitutes oppression and, therefore, warrants school choice as the mechanism for avoiding it is controversial. For example, a curriculum that portrays women as dutiful housewives is oppressive to feminists, whereas one that portrays them as career-oriented professionals is oppressive to moral conservatives. Such substantive disagreements aside, the basic rationale for school choice is the same.

In summary, the strong parental autonomy rationale takes two forms: libertarian and moral conservative. Libertarians support school choice, fearing the potential of public schools to indoctrinate per se; moral conservatives support school choice, fearing the potential of public schools to indoctrinate in the wrong way. The libertarian form possesses a "purity," as Peter Cookson (1994) says, that resolves the conflict between parental autonomy and equality of educational oppor-tunity[3] unambiguously in favor of the former. This very purity renders it untenable. The moral conservative form lacks such purity and cloaks the group's real reason for endorsing school choice, which is strategic, in the rhetoric of unconstrained parental autonomy.

THE MARKET RATIONALE

Where market rationales for schools of choice are straightforwardly lib-ertarian, they may be summarily dismissed for the reasons already given. Typically, however, market rationales add a utilitarian element that permits choice advocates to rest their case on something other than the overriding value of parental autonomy. In particular, choice is con-strued as instrumental, as working in the aggregate to form the invisible hand that generates the best overall consequences. This omnibus empir-ical claim makes the market rationale for school choice difficult to evalu-ate and serves to multiply the possibilities for distortion and obfusca-tion.

In this vein, many critics deny that market-driven school choice really works. Among the criticisms are that schools do the choosing, not parents and students; that choice is made on the basis of factors unre-lated to achievement; that choice exacerbates existing inequality of ac-cess and achievement; and, finally, that the underlying premise that funding makes little or no difference is false.[4] I think these kinds of criticisms are well taken, but they fall considerably short of carrying the day. Even if market-driven advocates were to concede them as generally correct, such criticisms can be dismissed as having to do with specific implementations of market-driven school choice rather than with the idea itself. (See, for example, Chubb & Moe, 1990.)

As other well-known debates in education illustrate—about track-ing and bilingual education, for instance—empirical disputes can be vir-tually interminable. One of the primary reasons for this is the debators' tendency to ignore deeper philosophical differences that warrant differ-ent interpretations of the empirical findings. In this vein, market-driven advocates have been able to cast the discussion in their own terms and have won a significant strategic advantage in the process. For, lost in a mountain of empirical claims and counterclaims about whether market-driven choice works has been a more straightforward and fundamental question: Is it consistent with the requirements of democracy?

The arguments I advance in the remainder of this section are di-rected largely against John Chubb and Terry Moe's (1990) influential

Politics, Markets and America's Schools, focusing especially on what I take to be their impoverished conception of democracy and their inconsistent use of student achievement as the criterion of school success. It should be observed that the criticisms I advance are broadly applicable to market-driven school choice. Although now some seven years old, Chubb and Moe's book still provides the most comprehensive defense of market-driven school choice available and is so frequently cited as to be the virtual Bible of market-driven choice advocates.

An Impoverished Conception of Democracy

Chubb and Moe (1990) are arrestingly unabashed in their identification of education with a consumer good. According to them, the problem with public schools is they fail to "please a clientele of parents and students," fail to "go out of business" if they don't, and fail to "appeal to specialized segments of consumer demand" (pp. 32–33). All of these failures they blame on "direct democratic control" and the fact that "conflict and disharmony are built into the system" (p. 34). They are immodest, to put it mildly, in proposing a solution:

> [W]e think reformers would do well to entertain the notion that choice *is* a panacea. . . . Choice is a self-contained reform with its own rationale and justification. It has the capacity *all by itself* to bring about the transformation that, for years, reformers have been seeking to engineer in myriad other ways. Indeed, if choice is to work to greatest advantage, it must be adopted *without* these other reforms, since the latter are predicated on democratic control and are implemented by bureaucratic means. Taken seriously, choice . . . is a revolutionary reform that introduces a new system of public education. (p. 217)

Now, what conception of democracy would have as a requirement eliminating "conflict and disharmony" about schooling? As Amy Gutmann (1987) observes,

> In a democracy, political disagreement is not something that we should generally seek to avoid. Political controversies over our educational problems are a particularly important source of social progress because they have the potential for educating so many citizens. (p. 5)

Chubb and Moe (1990) would blithely supplant democratic deliberation, negotiation, and compromise about schooling with a consumer model in which none of this has any point. But choice with respect automobiles, stoves, and refrigerators is not the same as choice with respect to schools (e.g., Pearson, 1993). Consumer choice is a *private* matter because it has relatively little impact on others.[5] By contrast, schooling is a *public* matter because it is intimately connected to fostering democracy. In virtue of this difference, whereas the distribution of consumer goods may be left to markets, the distribution of schooling must be sanctioned by defensible democratic procedures.

Chubb and Moe (1990) largely skirt this form of objection. They contend that schooling does not have to come under direct democratic control to serve the ends of democracy, and that in one grand democratic act we should dispense with it. This argument simply begs the question in favor of markets. Distributing automobiles via the market may not obstruct democracy, but it doesn't promote democracy either. At best, the market distribution of goods is merely *consistent* with democracy (it is also consistent with plutocracy, for instance).

Chubb and Moe (1990) consistently lump together democratic control, the imposition of "higher order values," and the evil demon of bureaucracy, all three of which they would eliminate by implementing their market-driven scheme. Their reasoning in this vein is breathtakingly ahistorical—as if bureaucracies just appeared of their own accord and began imposing their wills.[6] Missing from Chubb and Moe's analysis is the fact that many of the "higher order values" that are imposed on schools are the result of hard-fought political and legal battles. Consider *Brown v. Board of Education* (1954), the Education for All Handicapped Children Act (1974), the Bilingual Education Act (1968), and Title IX of the Education Amendments (1972). Exemplifying not the mere legal and political maneuvering of "special interests," the increased imposition of "higher order values" has been grounded in the morally justified goal of promoting equality of educational opportunity.

As it turns out, Chubb and Moe (1990) themselves do not altogether dispense with "higher order values." For example, although they contend that schools should be free to set their own admissions standards, they require that such standards be applied in a nondiscriminatory manner. They also suggest that students who are especially costly to educate, particularly at-risk students and students with disabilities, should be provided with more generous "scholarships" than regular students, so that schools will have an incentive to admit them. Chubb and Moe thus implicitly concede that equality of educational opportunity should be a legitimate constraint on their market-driven scheme.

But this concession is more apparent than real, which their claims about funding make quite clear. In particular, after putatively establishing that funding levels do not matter much [the received wisdom among neoconservatives since *A Nation at Risk* (1983)], they then proceed to address funding in their "scholarship" proposal in four important ways: (a) Scholarship amounts among poorer and wealthier districts should be equalized; (b) parents should be precluded from adding their own money to their children's scholarships; (c) special education and at-risk students should be provided with larger scholarships; (d) parents in local "taxing jurisdictions"[7] should be allowed to set their own scholarship amounts.

Notwithstanding their explicit arguments to the contrary, Chubb and Moe (1990) believe that funding does matter. If they didn't, recommendations such as these would be wholly incomprehensible. Apparently, however, they want to strictly avoid resisting the tide of opposition to increasing educational funding, and to redistributing it. Thus, whereas their official position is grounded in the *empirical claim* that increased funding is ineffective, their real position is grounded in the *political claim* that we should not be required to increase funding—unless, that is, we so choose. This interpretation is consistent with Chubb and Moe's first three recommendations, which, although conducive to equalizing educational opportunity, are optional. It is also consistent with the fourth (nonoptional) recommendation. In the context of other (nonoptional) recommendations they make—that schools should have a free hand to set their own admissions standards and their own expulsion policies—it insures that parents are free to spend more educational dollars on those children they *choose* to spend them on.

Save advocating "nondiscrimination requirements," then, Chubb and Moe (1990) do almost nothing to protect equality of educational opportunity. Given the (presumably nondiscriminatory) criteria for exclusion they mention—intelligence, interest, motivation, behavior, special needs (p. 222)—and one important criterion they fail to mention—lack of ability to pay—nondiscrimination can function in their scheme to protect equality of educational opportunity only in the most minimal and hollow way.

The Criterion of Success Problem

Chubb and Moe (1990) make their initial pitch for market-driven school choice in terms of maximizing the satisfaction of clients' preferences. Notice this is a much more inclusive criterion than academic achievement, for it includes anything and everything that "clients" might demand of schools. But, according to them, because investigating preferences would render their analysis unwieldy, they confine themselves to academic achievement as their criterion of success, as measured by standardized tests.

Here Chubb and Moe (1990) are open to the standard objection that relying so heavily on standardized test data yields a myopic analysis. But the problem goes much deeper than this. Why do Chubb and Moe believe it legitimate to focus on *any* uniform criterion of educational success? And why, in particular, is student achievement the appropriate touchstone? It is odd—inconsistent—for them to so roundly criticize the methods and aims of alternative school-reform proposals, particularly their putative tendency to restrict autonomy, and yet embrace the "measure of effectiveness that school reformers now rely on most" (p. 71). Chubb and Moe are caught in the following dilemma. If they maintain a consistent commitment to preference satisfaction as their criterion, then the question of whether school choice increases achievement is largely beside the point. If they adopt achievement as their criterion, they implicitly endorse a uniform aim for public education.

It seems unlikely that Chubb and Moe (1990) would want to make a thoroughgoing commitment to preference satisfaction as their criterion. By the nature of the case, schools that were chosen would win such a contest hands down, and few would take this to be an adequate defense of a school choice policy. In order for their overall argument to make sense, student achievement must be embraced as a uniform aim of education, and this greatly strains their appeal to the market. The market criterion, preference satisfaction, renders educational aims free to vary and individuals free to join with like-minded people in a marketplace of schools, in which democratic negotiation has no place. Why not simply measure preference satisfaction and then correlate *this* with school choice? The reason is that preference satisfaction is not the gold standard, achievement is. And the criterion of maximizing achievement renders a uniform educational aim that, as such, must be either subject to democratic negotiation or simply foisted on "clients" in a way that ignores "specialized segments of consumer demand."

When their argument is unmasked in this way, it is apparent that Chubb and Moe (1990) (and, I think, market advocates generally) merely provide a twist on the argument launched by *A Nation at Risk* (1983). They adopt two basic premises that have since become the received wisdom: (a) Achievement in U.S. public schools is so low as to threaten our national well-being, particularly economic, and (b) increased funding is not the answer. They then proffer the invisible hand of choice as the solution to the same old problem, cast in the terms of the same old criterion of success, using the same old economic framework.[8] They simply replace the heavy-handed accountability and retrenchment proposed in *A Nation at Risk* with the "panacea" of the market.

THE COMMUNITARIAN RATIONALE

Libertarian proponents of school choice see expanded choice as a good in itself, whereas market proponents see it as the key to economic efficiency. A third group of proponents—one that otherwise can be at vast political odds with the first two—sees expanded choice as required of community.

Among the general benefits communities provide to their members are a sense of self-worth, a feeling of belonging, and an opportunity to participate in social life. The communitarian[9] rationale focuses on the tremendous diversity that currently characterizes public school students and their families. It sees as wrong-headed—and no doubt morally objectionable—the practice of coping with this diversity by subjecting all students to cookie-cutter schools in order to inculcate in them the knowledge, skills, and values deemed appropriate by the powers that be. Instead a diverse collection of school communities must be permitted to flourish, and school choice is the mechanism by which this is to be achieved.

Choice advocates, such as Mary Anne Raywid (1990), contend that because the U.S. public education system is in such dire straights, school choice is an experiment well worth trying. More than this, Raywid is a strong advocate of school choice and charges its critics with ignoring the serious threat to the future of public education that now exists and with displaying a heavy bias toward the status quo. For her, school communities must be seen as integral wholes, built from the ground up. Any attempt to form community by add-ons to the schools we have is thus destined to fail (Raywid, 1994). In a related vein, choice advocates such as John E. Coons (1990) contend that any school reform that fails to provide historically oppressed and marginalized groups with the option of establishing their own school communities can result only in perpetuating their condition.

Now I find some accuracy in Raywid's (1990) charge that the variety of school choice that she and many others advocate has been misunderstood—indeed, caricatured—by its critics. But the charge may also be lodged in the other direction. Many critics of school choice, I among them, by no means wish to defend the status quo, nor, in response to Coons (1990), are we Platonic aristocrats who claim to know what is best for the unsophisticated masses. Instead, we are exceedingly wary of the bandwagon of school choice and who will wind up in the driver's seat as it continues to gather speed. Choice advocates like Raywid and Coons should be wary too.

The idea that schools should respond to diversity and should forge community, after all, is neither new nor the exclusive property of school choice advocates.[10] Furthermore, just what fostering community entails is a very complex question because "community" is a very complex concept. Political communities range from Dewey's (1981b) "Great Community" (which includes the entire nation) through states and municipalities to school districts. Other kinds of communities include collectives such as business persons, African Americans, and scholars, as well as individual schools and classrooms. One important question regarding any school reform measure that puts community at the center, then, is the community or communities it seeks to foster.

In the case of Coons's (1990) emphasis on nonoppression, providing a minimally decent education to all students constitutes one kind of requirement that schools should meet. Laying a school choice plan over this can only add but another layer of requirements—that must themselves be democratically negotiated. Insofar as school choice plans are supposed to enhance local democratic participation, ironically, these extra requirements must be both negotiated and enforced from a point at least one step removed from local schools. Why believe *these* negotiations will come out any better than negotiations to reform the schools we have, particularly when equalization of funding is one of the main sticking points in each case, when things such as transportation make choice schemes exceedingly costly (Levin, 1990), and when the political climate is strongly biased toward market solutions as against centralized oversight?

Suppose we could get the larger political community to agree to make important concessions regarding funding, transportation, and the like, so that there would be something approaching equality in the ability of different groups to establish nonoppressive schools. We still have the problem of what to do in the name of insuring that all schools develop democratic character. Coons (1990) admits that his proposal would inevitably result in the creation of schools he would not like, but he thinks democracy would be served overall. Well, is there a line here, or can any group set up any kind of school? How about "back to basics" schools that portray women exclusively in the role of caretakers of the family? Are regulations required here? How about schools that would exclude the disabled or certain religious and racial groups? Are regulations required here? How about Aryan Nation schools? Are regulations required here?

Coons (1990) is right to suggest that critics of school choice worry about its potential to undermine democracy and foster social fragmentation, but the reason he suggests for this worry—that the poor are not to be trusted to choose their own schools, whereas the rich are—is highly questionable. It is rhetorically effective, no doubt, to intimate that anyone who would claim that the poor are not in a good position to participate in school choice must be a hidebound aristocrat. It is also a simplistic dodge. Lack of information, lack of time, lack of transportation, lack of childcare, and lack of trust are among the reasons to worry that the poor have a compromised context of choice in comparison with the nonpoor (Wells, 1993; Wells & Crain, 1992). The poor and otherwise disadvantaged groups are also unlikely to be able to cut a deal with the rich and otherwise advantaged groups that would equalize their respective contexts of choice; and even if they could, the deal would be unstable and subject to revocation. Presumably, only the poor and otherwise disadvantaged really need expanded choice to escape a coercive, uniform curriculum imposed on them by the aristocrats. Why not (as I advocate later) limit choice to them?[11]

I endorse Raywid's (1994) call to build school-based communities, but in contrast to Raywid, I take schools of choice both to be a much less promising means to accomplish this and to pose a much greater threat to the historical aim of equalization. The much touted choice program in Manhattan's District 4 provides one example of how stratification can result from building school communities based on interests and talents, so that those students in the lowest strata are virtually abandoned (e.g., Kirp, 1992). In District 4 and elsewhere, school choice schemes have resulted in a zero-sum game; that is, increasing certain people's options has the consequence of decreasing others' (e.g., Henig, 1994; Pearson, 1993) and of increasing inequality (Elmore & Fuller, 1996). This is inevitable wherever there is competition for scarce social goods in the larger political community. Not even a majority of students can get into their first-choice school community, let alone all students. However much they diverge from market rationales in principle, school choice schemes that focus on building school communities while remaining hostile to or largely ignoring the need to also build broader political communities can be virtually indistinguishable from market schemes in their effects.

THE PRAGMATIC RATIONALE

In comparison to the three alternatives considered above, the pragmatic rationale regards the need (if not the prospects) for public schools to actively promote shared democratic ideals across communities as more central. For this reason, it is less ready to give up altogether on the idea of reforming the schools we have. Nonetheless, proponents of the pragmatic rationale exhibit varying degrees of skepticism regarding the suggestion that public education can be significantly improved by reforming the present system. They believe the public school system needs to be shaken up, and they see school choice as the way to do this.

School choice plans grounded in the pragmatic rationale are often described as employing ''controlled choice.'' As the name suggests, choice is permitted to operate only within boundaries set by more fundamental principles, equality of educational opportunity being central. Concrete principles include equalized funding, free transportation, prohibitions against resegregation, and nonexclusive admissions.

The problem with embracing this description is that all choices are ''controlled'' in the sense that they occur within a context that limits available options. Calls for choice in the policy arena—here we can add medical care to education—take this for granted and focus on carving out some measure of discretionary space for individuals and families. Within this space there is no coming to terms with others, no negotiation, because others' claims are precluded from encroaching on the individuals' and families' discretionary space. Compare my choice of whether to buy a chocolate or a vanilla ice cream cone. I would be a bit chagrined to be told that another person's interest or the public's interest was involved in my decision.

In this way, the market mentality has thoroughly insinuated itself into political discourse, including discourse about schools (Cookson, 1992). The description ''controlled choice'' thus has a distinct liability: It permits market-oriented proponents to cast the debate in their own language. The market mind-set is against control, whatever its form and whatever its justification. Because this mind-set frames everything on the model of consumer demand, it lacks the capacity to distinguish among justifications for policies. Even where the idea of government sponsorship and involvement is endorsed, everything is cast in the language of ''special interests,'' so that the economically based demands of tobacco growers are on a par with the morally based demands of bilingual educators.

We should start with the language of democracy and equality rather than with the language of the market.[12] We should stop engaging in a conversation that puts choice at the center and replace it with one that puts genuine participation at the center. Instead of asking, How much do we need to control choice?, we should ask instead, How can we best foster democracy? This places the burden of proof on those who would expand choice to show how this would not constrain or "control" democracy.

Defensible Choice Plans

As it turns out, rigidness, unresponsiveness, aloofness, ineffectiveness, and many of the other things for which choice advocates criticize the public schools are valid criticisms because all contribute to blunting participation (though I don't think school people should shoulder all, or even most, of the responsibility for this state of affairs). On the other hand, the participatory perspective rejects a monolithic school choice plan as the appropriate response. The key to a just system of public education is to ensure that any school community a student winds up in is a good one, and this requires a willingness to adapt to circumstances. So, to turn the tables, it is those who would altogether abandon efforts to reform the schools we have in favor of comprehensive choice schemes who may be tarred with the "one-size-fits-all" brush.

It should be observed here that choice in the form of private schools has long provided a safety valve—an escape from public education for those who seriously disagree with its mission on moral and political grounds (particularly religion-based), and likewise for those who have the means and desire to obtain a better education than they believe public schools can provide. Such a safety valve has not only given citizens a measure of discretion regarding their children's education; it has also been instrumental in establishing a majority coalition that has historically supported public schools by providing the dissatisfied and resolute with a way out.

This coalition is crumbling. Just why it is crumbling is open to debate, but I agree with those who blame the misinformation campaign that helps promote the agendas of right-wing reactionaries and market ideologues (see Bracey, 1994). In any case, if public education is to survive, it must respond to the current political realities. But expediency is not the only reason to expand choice. Again, choice advocates have a point about the public schools' being too standardized and too unresponsive to the diversity of interests, talents, cultures, and values.

Because choice plans can function to further equality and democracy only when combined with a commitment to create adequate public schools for everyone, it follows that building local school communities must be weighed against building wider democratic communities. This balancing is especially important in view of the opportunity gap school choice initiatives create between those students experiencing the best educational opportunities and those experiencing the worst. Below I discuss the ways in which means-tested vouchers, charter schools, and selective public schools may be implemented so as to satisfy these strictures.

Means-Tested Vouchers

Means-tested voucher plans provide low-income students with a way to exit inferior public schools. The ostensive aim of such plans is to close the opportunity gap between these students and higher income students.

One version of means-tested vouchers, the Private-School Parental Choice Plan, was implemented in Milwaukee in the 1990–91 school year. This plan provides students whose family incomes do not exceed 175% of the poverty level with the opportunity to attend the participating private schools.[13] For each voucher student, the state per pupil allocation is deducted from the state education budget and transferred to the designated private schools. Various restrictions apply. Participating private schools must be nonreligious and located within the city limits, limit voucher-student enrollment to 49% of all students, and meet specified academic progress and attendance standards. To be eligible, students must not have attended a private school within the previous year. Furthermore, the size of the program is restricted to a maximum of 1% of the total enrollment of the Milwaukee Public Schools.

The effectiveness of the program in terms of student achievement remains equivocal. By the measure of parental participation and support, however, it appears to be a resounding success (Wells, 1993). The participating private schools have not turned away low-achieving students or those with behavior problems. If anything, they have accepted a difficult group of students in these terms relative to the norm found in the public schools. The average number of years of education completed by participating parents (often single mothers) exceeds the district mean for all parents, and exceeds that of nonparticipating low-income parents by more.

The criticisms of the Milwaukee plan have been predictable (and not necessarily unsound for that reason). Chief among them is that the program gives participating private schools a competitive advantage over public schools. This perception results from the reduced requirements with which participating private schools must comply, particularly regarding teachers (they are permitted to pay teachers less and are required to provide fewer protections from firing) and special education (they are permitted to exclude students with disabilities where they lack appropriate facilities).

The threats to teachers and to students with disabilities are two features of the Milwaukee plan that cause concern. The probable response is that the plan responds to the abysmal condition of certain public schools and would be impossible if the nature of existing private schools were not taken into account. Granted, but this does not mean that more even-handed eligibility requirements cannot (and should not) be phased in over time.

That participating parents exhibit higher levels of education than nonparticipating parents is also a cause for concern. Whatever the reasons for this, the children of more highly educated parents enjoy an advantage over those with less well-educated parents. This further drives home the point that all public schools must be adequate and, accordingly, that choice plans can be only a small part of true educational reform.

A final cause for concern, prompted by all voucher plans, is that we've now taken our first step on a slippery slope and will inevitably slide to the bottom, where privatized schooling will be there to greet us. The only remedy for this problem is to demand significant restrictions, to keep equality of educational opportunity at the forefront, and to insist on continued efforts to improve existing public schools.

To be sure, each of these problems with the Milwaukee plan is significant. But in the present political context, and given the condition of many inner-city schools, no sufficient reason exists to dismantle the plan or to block experimenting with expanded plans that would also include public schools and private religious schools (Henig, 1994; Ravitch, 1994). In general, means-tested voucher plans are less problematic than comprehensive voucher plans, because they are limited in scope and protect the public schools better. They are also less costly and disruptive. Finally, as in Milwaukee, means-tested voucher plans promise some immediate relief to the group of citizens that has the best grounds for claiming injustice, so long as those citizens are willing and able to act.

Charter Schools

Unlike means-tested voucher plans, which have as their aim narrowing the opportunity gap, charter school plans have as their aim improving public education by providing competition within public school systems perceived to be hopelessly ossified and ineffective in their organizational structures and teaching practices. Charter schools[14] are organized within local school districts and subject to their approval. Ultimately, however, they are creatures of state boards, who also must approve their charters and who may overrule the decisions of local district boards, including denials or revocations. Additional features of charter school plans typically include nonsectarian programs, nonselective admissions, student performance standards, funding equivalent to the district per pupil allocation, a cap on the number of charter schools that can be formed, exemption from most state and local laws and regulations, and no allowance for transportation.

Charter schools are too new on the scene to have been evaluated very conclusively (Bierlein, 1996; Willis, 1995), but certain early findings are suggestive, several of which are potentially negative. For instance, there is little evidence that charter schools lead to improved student achievement and, even if such evidence existed, the fact that charter schools are generally small relative to ordinary public schools would confound interpretation. Further, although charter schools serve a racially and ethnically diverse population, many charter schools do not participate in the federal free/reduced-price food program, which suggests that they may be excluding low-income students. Thus (and contra Bierlein, 1996) charter schools may very well be "creaming," but on the basis of class rather than race or ethnicity.

On the other hand, a potentially positive finding is that parents are much more satisfied with their new charter schools and more engaged than they were with the public schools their children previously attended. But this should really come as no surprise. It follows almost automatically that parents so dissatisfied with the public schools that they were willing to expend the time and effort to establish a school of their own would be more satisfied with their creation. In this vein, a consistent finding regarding schools of choice across the spectrum of plans is that they engender greater parental satisfaction (e.g., Cookson, 1994; Henig, 1994; Wells, 1993).

In addition to the criticisms above, two major complaints about means-tested vouchers also apply to charter schools: They set up unfair terms of competition with ordinary public schools, and they pose a threat to teachers. Charter schools, unlike those in the Milwaukee plan, cannot point to the existing practices and requirements of private schools as an excuse, because charter schools are established within existing public school systems. These criticisms are not all that telling, however, so long as the number of charter schools that can be created remains limited by a relatively restrictive cap.

I seriously doubt that charter schools will do anything to improve the quality of U.S. education, particularly with respect to the opportunity gap, but neither will they do anything to harm it (barring any significant changes in the present requirements and limitations). In my view, charter schools currently exemplify a reasonable political compromise.

Selective Public Schools

Selective public school admissions are frequently viewed as unjust, and many choice plans rightly preclude them. Indeed, I criticized them myself in the case of Manhattan District 4. But imagine a school district in which all schools are adequate and, as a consequence, no zero-sum game is being played at the expense of the least advantaged. Under these circumstances (and I am sure some school districts qualify), it would be acceptable in my view to establish a limited number of specialized schools that selected students based on talent—in art, dance, and science, for instance. Although such a system would require free transportation and other kinds of support to aid low-income students and to avoid segregation by race and ethnicity, and would have to insure that the curriculum placed sufficient emphasis on the participatory educational ideal, selecting on the basis of talent would not be inherently unjust. Of course, this hypothetical district might not establish any specialized schools whatsoever, or it might assign students to them on the basis of interest alone. Neither of these options would be unjust either.

Here it should be observed that, consistent with a threshold conception of equality of educational opportunity (see Chapter 2), justice does not require eliminating the opportunity gap altogether. Different people place a different value on education relative to other social goods and allocate their discretionary time, effort, and resources accordingly. It is a mistake to try to prevent them from acting on these differences. It is not a mistake, however, to try to prevent the unfair advantages that result from allowing the opportunity gap to become too large.

Consider a different kind of example of selective admissions. Imagine that a proposal was put forward to create a Spanish–English bilingual school in a community with a relatively large number of Spanish-speaking children and that parents, especially Spanish-speakers, were actively recruited to take advantage of this option. Imagine further that although Whites could be admitted, if space were available, the primary admissions criterion was Spanish as a first language.

Unlike in the preceding example, the justification for such a school would not to be to celebrate, encourage, and reward special talents. It would more likely be a response to the need to make the best use of scarce bilingual resources by concentrating personnel in one school or the need to create a "critical cultural mass" so that Spanish-speaking students would be made comfortable by familiar faces, norms, and a collective history and, in turn, would have their sense of self ratified and bolstered. Like the preceding example, such a proposal is not inherently unjust simply because it denies some students their first choice. As I intimated before, choices are always subject to control. The crucial question is, To what end?

CONCLUSION

The rush to school choice results from a somewhat restricted view of what "school reform" should encompass, because true reform cannot be understood apart from the democratic procedures and principles that govern it.[15] Indeed, the penchant to abstract schools from the broader political context and then to call for reform through the mechanism of choice deserves a name: the *fallacy of misplaced radicalness*. This kind of thinking follows in the wake of the now pervasive perception that welfare-state liberalism has proved an unmitigated failure. General examples include measures such as cutting persons' public assistance in order to help them lift themselves up by their bootstraps and implementing mandatory prison sentences in order to reduce crime. In each case, radical policies are aimed at the visible tip of the iceberg, and underlying (and invisible) socioeconomic structures go unaddressed.

The same may be said of school choice that sees itself as anything more than a modest add-on to much more far-reaching school reform. It is exceedingly difficult to imagine how the radicalism that is school choice can remedy the kind of grossly inadequate schooling that many U.S. children experience. When erected atop fundamentally unjust and undemocratic political-economic arrangements, school choice schemes have no hope of providing anything even approaching a general solution for what ails the U.S. public education system.

The clamor for school choice, like the clamor for more rigorous standards and assessments, is a diversion from the real problems facing public education, as well as the likely remedies. But school choice is the more potentially damaging and irreversible of the two. However anemic in its requirements for equal opportunity and flawed in its conception of the curriculum, at least the standards and assessment movement incorporates the ideas that public education has a responsibility to impart some shared knowledge and values and that it should be held accountable for doing so. By contrast, the school choice movement, so dominated by a consumerist mentality, promises a mysterious "deus ex machina, sent by the gods of market forces" (Henig, 1994, p. 116). Standards and assessment can play a role, but one limited to providing information on the model of an educational *Consumer Reports*. In such a system, parents of children in the public schools who otherwise might be committed to eliminating educational inequality would be faced with the option of either making their children into martyrs by sending them to inferior schools or scrambling to insure that their children wouldn't be losers in the zero-sum game. Citizens without children in the public schools would be excluded from any legitimate say in how schools should respond to the ''specialized segments of consumer demand'' associated with schools' true ''clients.'' Over time, I fear, the general commitment to public education could only erode further.

The only way to prevent school choice from undermining public education is to forge political communities that see it as a very limited solution to the real problem that infects our school system and our democracy: vast inequality of educational opportunity. Political communities are likely to see things in this way only if their members share the view that we exist within a scheme of social cooperation that must be structured so as to include all citizens, insuring that all participate in its institutions and enjoy its various goods.

Though always subject to controversy in the details and always falling considerably short, public schooling has long been charged with the role of *fostering* some such participatory ideal. This ideal is now under fundamental attack by school choice advocates who—whether adopting the rationale of fostering liberty, unleashing the market, or building communities—would assign to public schooling the role of merely *responding* to non-negotiable demands. This state of affairs gives considerable credence to Peter Cookson's (1994) characterization of the school choice controversy as ''the struggle for the soul of American education.''

CHAPTER 8

Conclusion

[J]ustice belongs to the highest class of good things which are worth having not only for their consequences, but much more for their own sakes.

—*Plato,* The Republic

We cannot preserve a sense of justice and all that implies while at the same time holding ourselves ready to act unjustly should doing so promise some personal advantage. A just person is not prepared to do certain things.

—*John Rawls,* A Theory of Justice

Plato and Rawls (1971) agree that a commitment to justice must be securely implanted within the character of the citizens of a just state. The only alternative in their eyes is the patent injustice associated with unbridled self-interest, and the unrest, instability, and brutish form of social life that follows in its wake. They agree as well that the design of the education system—particularly what opportunities it provides, and to whom—is central to the design of the just state.

Of course, Plato and Rawls (1971) diverge dramatically on the specific conception of justice to which they believe a commitment should attach. Plato advocated an aristocracy, to be ruled by his properly educated philosopher-kings. The accompanying conception of justice required everyone to accept his or her biologically determined station in life. The principle of equality, accordingly, had no place—indeed, equality was the clear mark of *in*justice. Rawls, by contrast, is strongly egalitarian. He views equality as part and parcel of any adequate conception of justice, and he extends equality so as to include equality of opportunity in general and equality of educational opportunity in particular. Rawls articulates the point of departure shared by liberal-egalitarians today.

Now, I would count various leftists, postmodernists, communitarians, and care theorists as fellow egalitarian travelers, who are at least as much at odds with Plato and his modern-day disciples[1] as I am. As such, I do not disagree with them in characterizing the present condition of public education as woefully unjust as well as undemocratic. Nor do I disagree that libertarian and utilitarian forms of liberalism are irredeemably flawed. Nor, finally, do I disagree that the prevailing formal and compensatory interpretations of equality of educational opportunity have serious problems. I do disagree, however, that these frameworks provide the only ways to interpret liberalism and equality of educational opportunity, and that the liberal project is therefore hopelessly flawed. Let me review the alternative interpretation I have staked out in this book.

Recall that liberal-egalitarianism may be distinguished from its libertarian and utilitarian competitors largely in terms of its conception of distributive justice. Libertarianism maintains a strong presumption against any form of involuntary distribution of social goods (goods such as health, education, and income, for instance). Utilitarianism, by contrast, rejects this presumption and requires actively manipulating social arrangements so as to insure that distributions of goods serve to maximize benefits. For its part, liberal-egalitarianism also requires manipulating social arrangements, but, unlike utilitarianism, it places constraints on the shape that the distribution of benefits can take. In particular, social arrangements must be designed so as to tend toward equality in the distribution of benefits. To this end, the effects of factors that are ''arbitrary from a moral point of view,'' for example, who one's parents happen to be, must be mitigated—if necessary, at the expense of maximization. The distributions resulting from the operation of markets (libertarianism's distributive principle) similarly must be held in check.

Liberal-egalitarianism has dominated the liberal tradition (perhaps political theory in general) since the publication of Rawls's (1971) celebrated *A Theory of Justice*. Of course, this general perspective has not gone unchallenged, as I have observed numerous times before. Among the general charges advanced against it are that it is paternalistic and oppressive as well as undemocratic. This is so because liberal-egalitarianism identifies the disadvantaged in terms of the relatively low share of social goods they possess. It then sets about the task of eliminating the identified disadvantages by implementing various compensatory social programs, educational and otherwise. All of this is conceived so as to require little or no input from those most affected. Liberal-egalitarianism thus presupposes that the social goods to be distributed, as well as the distribution procedures, are uncontested. But, contrary to this presupposition, these goods and procedures in fact reflect the values and interests of those who have been and continue to be in charge.

Consider, for example, a thoroughly sexist curriculum with which girls, but not boys, have great difficulty. It is hardly a solution to provide girls more help in mastering *this* curriculum so as to remove their putative disadvantage.

So far as I can tell, this problem is taken to sound the death knell of liberal education theory by its critics, and perhaps it would if liberals offered nothing by way of response. But contrary to the conclusion one might draw from the way in which liberalism is nowadays so often caricatured and then dismissed, liberals have by no means either ignored this kind of criticism or thrown up their hands in defeat. Instead, they have fashioned a general response, conceding to the critics that too sharp a distinction between democracy and justice has characterized liberal-egalitarianism of the past. Liberal-egalitarians then go on to shift the interpretation of equality from an emphasis on the distribution of predetermined goods to an emphasis on democracy. Given this revision, justice requires giving all people an effective voice in negotiating goods and defining their own needs, particularly members of groups that have been historically excluded. This shift to a "participatory paradigm"[2] renders justice, democracy, and equality so tightly intertwined that it is impossible to have any one of them without having them all. To paraphrase Will Kymlicka (1991), "it only makes sense to invite people to participate in" schooling "(or for people to accept that invitation) if they are treated as equals. . . . And that is incompatible with defining people in terms of roles they did not shape or endorse" (p. 89).

This general liberal framework provides the participatory interpretation of equality of educational opportunity that I have employed throughout with its meaning and rationale. Recall that the participatory interpretation was fleshed out in terms of the three related requirements: the "participatory educational ideal" (the general ideal to which education in a democracy should aspire), the "virtue of recognition" (a central character trait that should be fostered in all democratic citizens), and the "principle of nonoppression" (the procedural embodiment of the virtue of recognition). Although these requirements can no doubt be made more precise than I have made them, there are definite limits to how far this can go. We would do well here to heed Aristotle's advice to look only "for as much precision . . . as the subject matter allows" (in Bambrough, trans., 1963, p. 287). These requirements must remain sensitive to history and to prevailing social conditions, including, of course, the kind and amount of education required to be a full-fledged participant in the democratic process. Vague as they might be in the abstract, these requirements nonetheless provide sufficient guidance to make a huge difference in the education policies they sanction, compared to other general frameworks that may be adopted.The analyses in the preceding chapters—of gender, multiculturalism, standards and testing, segregation, and schools of choice—should drive this point home.

I believe there are compelling *philosophical* reasons for embracing the kind of *radical* liberal theory I have developed and applied in the preceding pages, and, along with it, the vocabulary of equality and opportunity. Chief among these is that this form of liberalism avoids the difficulties that beset the frameworks of postmodernists, communitarians, and care theorists regarding how to make sense of justice. For lack of a better description, there are also *strategic* reasons for embracing the vocabulary of liberalism. In particular, these are especially bad times (not that there are any good times) to be labeling the quest for equality of educational opportunity as too abstract, too uncaring, too aloof from community, and inherently oppressive. For this plays into the hands of the current attack on public education from the New Right, who are more than ready to offer an alternative vocabulary.[3]

Consider that equality of educational opportunity has been identified as the chief culprit in "dumbing down" the curriculum (Murray & Herrnstein, 1994, chaps. 17 and 18). In its place should be excellence, competition, and the same high standards and expectations for all. Of course, certain critics of the ideal of equality of educational opportunity—Noddings (1992), for instance—are at least as opposed to mindless competition, "world-class standards," and the same standards and expectations for all as I am. But is it a promising strategy to combine opposition to these requirements with Noddings's (1993b) argument that "excellence" ought to replace "equality" as the guiding educational ideal? Shouldn't one pay careful attention to the kinds of views with which "excellence" has been associated in contemporary education policy debates? True, the principle of equality of educational opportunity has itself been used to rationalize injustice, particularly under its formal interpretation. But, in my estimation, it is better to reveal these rationalizations for what they are than to capitulate to those who would abandon the quest for equality of educational opportunity. Overall, this quest has been a driving force for progressive educational change.

Consider schools of choice once again, particularly the immense trust they place in individual parents and communities. This level of trust seems altogether unwarranted in light of the present political climate. For example, Senator Phil Gramm, a leader in the Republican Party and once a serious contender for his party's nomination for President, responded to a television interviewer's question about what choice means specifically for special education with a question of his own: Do you think bureaucrats in Washington care more about handicapped children than people in local communities do? (MacNeil, 1995). Later in the interview, Gramm seemed to imply the wrong answer to this question, saying it would be perfectly all right with him to cut funding for special education (and increase it for the gifted), if that is what local communities chose to do.

Gramm's question should have been countered with another: Wasn't depending on local communities the modus operandi before litigation and legislation of the 1970s required local communities to do much more to educate children with disabilities? Persons with disabilities are in an especially vulnerable position because they are such a small minority within individual communities (Gutmann, 1987), and it is by no means clear that local communities can be trusted to respond in the right way now any more than they could be trusted to do so two decades ago.

This is no mere abstract, theoretical worry. The much ballyhooed Milwaukee voucher plan,[4] for instance, permits participating schools to exclude special education students, and the plan is under expansion (Lindsay, 1995). At the federal level, funding for portions of the Individuals with Disabilities Education Act (the successor legislation of the Education for All Handicapped Children Act, PL 94–142) has been held hostage to a national voucher plan (Pitsch, 1995a). Finally, in my own community, a group of parents (in collaboration with the newly elected school board that ran on a plank advocating rigorous academics) succeeded in establishing an elite charter school that de facto excludes most special education students on the basis of standardized test scores.

The reason that these kinds of educational reforms have gained such broad support is probably not that people are in general hopelessly calloused and totally self-interested (though some clearly are). More likely, it is because the onslaught of criticism from all sides has pushed the essential requirements of the just society from view. Justice can be achieved only under arrangements in which overarching principles prevent community allegiances, loyalty to family, and personal interests from running amuck, and only when people are motivated to act in accordance with such principles by a sense of justice that is fundamental to their identities.

Under cover of the vocabulary of excellence, economic competitiveness, parental choice, community control, and the magic of the market, pressures to segregate students, to subject them to "world-class" standards, to hold them accountable with tests, and the like, are increasing. The best way to resist the regressive policies this vocabulary spawns is by appeal to the vocabulary of the liberal-democratic tradition. Because this vocabulary is familiar to the U.S. citizenry, it holds the most promise for effectively challenging those who avow a commitment to democracy, justice, and equality of educational opportunity, and for inducing them to live up to what these ideals require. For the commitment to these ideals rings hollow in the absence of a further commitment to what is necessary to bring them about: an educational system that provides all children with educational opportunities worth wanting.

Notes

CHAPTER 1

1. That no interpretation of equality of educational opportunity can be totally divorced from the criterion of educational results is a claim I elaborate in Chapter 2.

2. As Gutmann (1987) observes, whether explicitly and coherently or not, all education policy proposals presuppose some kind of political theory.

3. The distinction between "real" and "bare" opportunities is from Daniel Dennett (1984).

4. I describe these theories in detail in Chapter 3. Here it is sufficient to observe that liberal-egalitarians hold, against libertarians, that equality must check excessive freedom and, indeed, equality is required for freedom to be widely enjoyed; they hold, against utilitarians, that equality requires checks on the shape of the distributions of society's goods, including education. The total good produced should not be the only consideration.

5. The concept of a "context of choice" is developed by Will Kymlicka (1991).

6. The labels *humanist* and *gynocentric* are from Iris Marion Young (1990b, chap. 5); *liberal* and *relational* are from Nel Noddings (1990).

7. The concept of "recognition" is from Charles Taylor (1994). My interpretation differs from his, however.

8. Here *liberal* in its popular usage should be distinguished from liberal political theory.

9. Incidentally, I have been labeled a left-winger in print by at least one commentator. See Schrag (1992).

CHAPTER 2

1. The threshold interpretation of equality of educational opportunity is primarily from Gutmann (1987).

2. This section title is inspired by John Rawls (1985), "Justice as Fairness: Political, Not Metaphysical." My argument is at most loosely related to the argument Rawls advances.

3. In addition to O'Neill, the following, to name a few, also exemplify the

received view: Ralph Page (1976), Robert Ennis (1976), Nicholas Burbules and Ann Sherman (1979), Nicholas Burbules, Brian Lord, and Ann Sherman (1982), and Christopher Jencks (1988).

4. This concept is from Will Kymlicka (1991).

5. I use Robert Nozick's (1974) view from *Anarchy, State, and Utopia* throughout this section to characterize libertarian political theory.

6. One way for meritocratic utilitarians to justify this inegalitarian result would be to argue that the principles of maximizing productivity and merit dovetail in such a way that awarding educational opportunities on the basis of economically valuable skills also increases economic productivity. But this response faces a significant obstacle. Norman Daniels (1991) has shown that the principle of maximizing economic productivity and the principle of merit may conflict. Put simply, the most economically productive arrangement may require assigning individuals to positions for which they are not best suited (or most meritorious). For example, an individual might make a better physician than schoolteacher relative to other individuals in each pool, in which case the principle of merit would dictate that he or she be permitted to pursue a career in medicine. But if minimally competent teachers were in short supply in comparison to physicians, the principle of maximizing productivity would dictate that the individual pursue a career in teaching. Thus the principle of merit would dictate one thing and the principle of maximizing productivity another.

7. But for a further complication in liberal theory, see, for example, Kenneth Strike's (1991) discussion of the difference between liberal and democratic theorists.

8. Very briefly, a threshold provides a substantive target (versus a mere procedural rule) and fits with my intuition that above a certain level, the benefits that may be derived from additional education are subject to a strong version of the law of diminishing returns. In addition, educational attainment cannot be redistributed in the same way as income, for example. For more on the idea of an educational threshold, see, for example, Gutmann (1987) and Curren (1995).

9. Utilitarianism is also typically a compensatory view, but it has additional problems already discussed.

10. This isn't merely a point about effective political rhetoric. Rawls (1971) suggests that an appeal to what citizens are already committed to is a starting point for political philosophy. But see especially Michael Walzer (1987) and Charles Taylor (1995, chap. 3) for an explicit defense of this approach to doing political philosophy.

CHAPTER 3

1. This general kind of argument is developed more fully by, for example, Young (1990b, chap. 2) and Connell (1987).

2. The labels *humanist* and *gynocentric* are attributable to Iris Marion Young (1990b, chap. 5), 73–91; *liberal* and *relational* to Nel Noddings (1990).

3. This was the basic thrust of at least the early work of Sadker and Sadker (1986).

4. This is not to say that Gilligan herself would embrace gynocentrism.

5. As I make clear later, Noddings (1993b) actually would prefer to reorient the discussion away from educational equality altogether, in favor of educational excellence.

6. Young (1990b, chap. 5) identifies three particular dangers. The first is encouraging a "disturbing essentialism," where by *essentialism* Young means "an account that theorizes women as a category with a set of essential attributes" (p. 87). Reproductive biology and the role of mothering are standard examples. According to Young, this encourages looking at gender differences as static, as a "relation of inside and outside" (p. 88).

The second way gynocentric feminism threatens to rationalize and perpetuate women's oppression is that by celebrating the value of feminine experience and approaches to living in the attempt to rescue women from being viewed as "victims, weak, passive, and only partial human beings" (Young, 1990b, chap. 5, p. 88), it renders the claim that women have been dominated difficult to maintain. "Such a way of conceptualizing male domination," writes Young, "mutes the outrage against injustice that humanist feminism exhibits because [humanist feminism] claims that women are not simply devalued, but also damaged, by male domination" (p. 88).

The final way gynocentric feminism threatens to rationalize and perpetuate women's oppression is that it can feed into antifeminist backlash. Insofar as it celebrates feminine virtues and rejects masculine ones, it serves to reinforce gender stereotypes and separateness, carving out separate spheres for the operation of each. This has the consequence of placing women outside the male-dominated sites of "power, privilege, and recognition" of which they want no part. As a consequence, Young contends, "feminism can be only a moral position of critique rather than a force for institutional change" (p. 89).

7. As indicated previously, Noddings (1990) uses *liberal* and *relational,* respectively, for *humanist* and *gynocentric.* Otherwise, her way of distinguishing these two kinds of feminisms is virtually the same as Young's.

8. Noddings cites Green (1983, 1991). Interestingly, as I understand Green, his position is closer to mine than to Noddings's. In particular, excellence and equality are complementary rather than exclusive. That is, equality (particularly formal equality) must be conjoined with excellence (some substantive educational goal(s)) in the overall design of the education system. This reasoning parallels the reasoning associated with the call for a substantive educational threshold, to which Green himself makes reference.

9. Gutmann proposes to do this, at least partly, through the mechanism of affirmative action. In her view, under present conditions, women have a qualification that men lack as prospective school administrators, namely, an increased capacity to blunt the repression of girls in schools. This general form of argument is borrowed from Ronald Dworkin (1977), who applies it to racial preferences.

10. The "morality of principles" is borrowed from John Rawls (1971) and has a quite specific meaning. It is identified with the highest form of moral development and requires that individuals have a direct attachment to moral principle rather than to concrete individuals and relationships (the latter characterizes the "morality of association").

11. The "morality of association" is also from Rawls (1971).

CHAPTER 4

1. As he mentions in the acknowledgments of *Cultural Literacy*, Hirsch (1988) was supported and encouraged by well-known conservatives such as Diane Ravitch, Chester Finn, and William Bennett.

2. Lisa Delpit (1993), for instance, argues that although schooling clearly needs to change in its treatment of Black children, in the meantime, it is clearly in their interests to learn the "code" of privilege and power.

3. Numerous examples exist in political theory, but for specific applications of critical theory to education, see Robert Young (1990) and Nicholas Burbules (1993). For an application of liberalism, see Kenneth Strike (1991). The arguments of this book, of course, are also in the liberal tradition.

4. See, for example, Lather (1991b), Giroux (1988), and McLaren (1988).

5. Several commentators maintain, rightly in my view, that pragmatists such as Dewey and James appreciated the antifoundational thrust of postmodernism long ago but took this as the point of departure for ongoing philosophical work. See, for example, Bernstein (1996).

6. Gutmann (1987) may well have a response to this line of criticism, for she employs "nonrepression" in an unusually expansive way. Her analysis of "sexist" education provides a specific illustration. In the name of nonrepression she advocates affirmative action for women seeking educational administration posts in order to counteract the general sexist climate where men possess a disproportionate share of authority. As Gutmann uses it, then, "repression" is not confined to overt silencing but may also be found in institutional arrangements as well as in the hidden curriculum. This stretches the ordinary meaning of "nonrepression" a goodly distance. I prefer to avoid this difficulty by supplanting *nonrepression* with *nonoppression*.

7. If we use linguistic minorities served by Title VII programs as a stand-in for cultures, which renders a quite conservative estimate, there are 198. (See U.S. Department of Education, 1995.)

8. Here I am bracketing the issue of gender, a topic already considered in detail in Chapter 3.

9. This, of course, is a pervasive theme of Dewey's work and has been rediscovered of late. It is resonant in virtually all current educational thought that sets itself up against the melting pot idea. The task of effecting it is made all the more daunting by the standards and assessment movement in U.S. education (the topic of Chapter 6). For an ostensive *partial* canon tends to become a de facto *full* canon, which crowds out anything that falls outside its scope (read:

anything that is not tested). "Recognition" is rendered superficial, devolving into making a modicum of time available in the school calendar for activities such as international food days.

10. See, for example, Young (1990a) and Kymlicka (1991, 1995) for defenses of formalized group rights.

11. See, for example, Habermas (1994) and Appiah (1994) for critiques of formalized group rights.

12. This tripartite distinction is from Ogbu and Matute-Bianchi (1986).

13. See, for example, Noddings (1993a).

14. This is the crux of the argument in *Wisconsin v. Yoder* (1972).

15. Kymlicka (1995) approaches this general problem by distinguishing between what he calls "external protections" and "internal restrictions." "External protections" are required to protect the context of choice provided by certain communities from being overwhelmed and destroyed by the larger political-economic community. Kymlicka endorses external protections as necessary for autonomy. (An example is special land rights for Native Americans.) "Internal restrictions," by contrast, are limitations placed by a community on its own members, also in the name of self-preservation. Kymlicka rejects internal restrictions as inconsistent with autonomy. (An example is regulation of religious belief.)

A liberal, Kymlicka nonetheless concedes the importance of community in providing a background of values and practices that render individual autonomy meaningful. He also concedes that external protections can sometimes serve as the justification for internal restrictions, and that, when they do, an appropriate response is problematic. This problem seems to be especially acute in the case of Amish schooling. Indeed, Kymlicka's distinction between external protections and internal restrictions seems to break down altogether. For internal restrictions on what Amish children are to be exposed to and how they are to think are imposed in the name of protecting the community from the outside world. If this schooling accomplishes its aims, then even if, as adults, Amish community members are not subject to internal restrictions on their autonomy, their schooling will have rendered them neither disposed nor equipped to exercise it to entertain alternative ways of life.

In my view, Kymlicka's analysis breaks down because of the special role of schooling in preparing children for adulthood and points to a conundrum: To foster multiculturalism (and nonoppression) at the community level, Amish children forgo multicultural (and nonoppressive) education at the individual level.

16. Kymlicka (1995) defends such a special obligation as applying across social and political institutions.

CHAPTER 5

1. A common variation of this scheme nowadays is to track children in terms of specific subjects rather than generally. See, for example, Hallinan (1994a).

2. Oakes (1987) gives this view as an explanation of why tracking continues to have a strong following. See Hallinan (1994a) for an example of an educational researcher who endorses this argument.

3. In a general way, this justification for tracking (or "sorting") has been with us for a long time and has been much discussed. See especially Spring (1989), and Oakes (1985, chap. 2).

4. Oakes's work (1985, 1990, 1994) is one clear exception. However, even she fails to sufficiently pursue the import of the democratic aims of education in addressing the issue of tracking.

5. I have more to say about the issue of funding in Chapter 7.

6. This is the position of Adler and associates (1982) in the *Paideia Proposal*.

7. This is a view I once heard advanced (and unabashedly) by a Denver economist.

8. Dewey's (1938, chap. 3) notion of "collateral learning" is germane here. See also Noddings (1992).

9. These rationales are to be found in various places. For an explicit statement of both, see Fetterman (1988).

10. This is much discussed, but see especially Maker and Schiever (1989) and Richert (1991).

11. At least this seems to be true in this particular case, which is not to say that an integration/compensatory approach for children such as Amy Rowley is uniformly endorsed.

12. See the case, "Pulling the Plug on Children With Profound Disabilities?" in Howe and Miramontes (1992, pp. 37–41).

CHAPTER 6

1. A test could conceivably be biased against a group in the absence of differential test performance between the group in question and other groups, though I am not familiar with such cases.

2. I am skeptical that assessment can drive curriculum and instruction without also shaping them to serve assessment. George Madaus (1994) shares my skepticism. He employs the delightful example of the manner in which the invention of tomato-picking machines led to the development of tough-skinned, less tasty tomatoes.

3. I find quite baffling the suggestion that providing students with different ways of demonstrating the same desired performance helps with the problem of equity, a suggestion made by, for example, Linda Darling-Hammond (1994) and Robert Rothman (1994). If the performance (construct) is itself biased, then the means of measuring it are moot. Furthermore, it is odd to suggest that different kinds of performance assessments can zero in on the same performance (construct), or it is at least odd that we would want them to. Isn't one of the virtues of performance assessment its relatively direct tie to the richness and peculiarities of given kinds of activities?

4. The distinction between hypothetical and categorical validity judgments is inspired by Kant's distinction between hypothetical and categorical imperatives, which correspond, respectively, to prudential, means-ends ought statements (e.g., "If you want to be rich, then you ought to X") versus moral ought statements (e.g., "You ought not X"). I do not mean to suggest by this usage that statements of the form "X use of testing is categorically valid" may not involve a good deal of controversy. (It is perhaps worth noting here that the claim "The earth revolves about the sun," although once very controversial, was consistently advanced categorically.)

5. For a discussion of similar issues regarding the validity of educational research, see Howe (1985) and Howe and Eisenhart (1990).

6. Like Madaus (1994), I believe that the shift from *testing* to *assessment* does not substantially change things. The overriding issues remain the broader social context in which testing (assessment) is employed and the purposes to which it is put.

7. See Chapter 2 for a more elaborate discussion of this point.

8. Formalist and compensatory schemes typically do not come in pure forms. For example, *America 2000* (1991), which is formalist in its emphasis, advocates increased funding for Head Start. In the real world of educational policy, the formalist-compensation distinction is one of degree that depends on the relative tilt toward one or the other end of the spectrum.

9. In this way Rawls (1971) may be interpreted as endorsing a form of meritocracy. See, for example, Daniels (1991).

10. This assessment practice was promoted long ago by Dewey. Recently, in addition to Noddings (1992), prominent policy/testing analysts such as Linda Darling-Hammond (1994) and George Madaus (1994) have also endorsed it.

11. The "valued added" interpretation was introduced to me by Richard Elmore (1994) in his comments at an AERA symposium. I do not mean to suggest that Elmore necessarily endorses this as the way that opportunity to learn ought to be interpreted.

12. Those interpretations focused almost exclusively on a formal interpretation of equality of educational opportunity. (See U.S. House of Representatives, 1994a.) If anything, the situation has deteriorated. The Clinton administration softened its support for opportunities to learn, apparently in order to keep *Goals 2000* afloat in the face of congressional threats to withdraw funding. See Pitsch (1995b).

CHAPTER 7

1. Such a view is often attributed to John Stuart Mill. See, for example, Cookson (1994).

2. Harry Vickery, head of the Moral Majority of New Jersey in the mid-1980s, represents the fundamentalist Christian view as committed to a day in which a "benevolent dictator"—the Christian God—will "enforce righteous-

ness.'' He and other leaders of fundamentalist Christians—for example, Jimmy Lee Swaggert and Timothy LaHaye—see gaining control of the public schools as an important part of achieving this aim. See Films for the Humanities (1988); also see Cox (1995).

3. See, for example, James Coleman (1990) for a statement of this conflict.I should note that although I endorse Coleman's way of framing the problem, I do not share his enthusiasm for schools of choice.

4. See, for example, Amy Stuart Wells and Robert L. Crain (1992), Jeffrey Henig (1994), Judith Pearson (1993), and David L. Kirp (1992) for discussions of these general points. For discussions more specific to the funding issue, see Gerald Bracey (1992), Ernest House (1991), Joel Spring (1984), Larry V. Hedges, Richard D. Laine, and Rob Greenwald (1994), and David Berliner and Bruce Biddle (1995).

5. This is arguable, of course, and is a matter of degree. For example, emissions standards for automobiles restrict the range of consumer choice in order to promote the public good.

6. This point was suggested to me by Pearson (1993). It is also noteworthy here that growth in teaching staff per student has far outpaced growth in administrators per student. Also see John Witte (1990).

7. This is what school districts become after their other prerogatives are stripped away (Chubb & Moe, 1990).

8. See Strike (1984) for a discussion of the utilitarian framework employed in *A Nation at Risk* (1983).

9. Though quite broad in its usage, ''communitarian'' has nonetheless come to be associated with a particular neo-Aristotelian position in political philosophy (e.g., MacIntyre, 1981). I should make clear that I do not have this specific position in mind.

10. These are major themes in John Dewey's work and have been recently urged by prominent educational theorists such as Nel Noddings (1992), Jane Roland Martin (1992), and Amy Gutmann (1987). Each roundly criticizes the curriculum, teaching methods, and organization of the schools we have for failing to mesh with the talents and interests of a large number of students, and thus failing to draw them into community, failing to foster the intellectual skills and character traits required for living in community, failing to spark and maintain an interest in schooling, and, ultimately, failing to provide them with a decent education.

None of these thinkers, however, sees school choice as the answer. For historical reasons, in the case of Dewey, and reasons of emphasis, in the case of Noddings and Martin, these three are largely silent on the issue. Other things they say, however, suggest a general view, which is that public schools should take the students they get and then forge school communities accordingly. For her part, Gutmann (1987) is explicitly critical.

11. In his earlier collaboration with Sugarman (Coons & Sugarman, 1978), Coons endorses this kind of limited-choice plan but expresses a strong preference for comprehensive plans.

12. Cookson (1994) employs the notion of "justice-driven" schools of choice in an effort to redirect the conversation in the same way that I do.

13. In this way, Milwaukee's Private-School Parental Choice Plan is a limited voucher plan.

14. The description of charter schools depends heavily on Bierlein and Mulholland (1994).

15. This is one of the rare points on which I agree with Chubb and Moe (1990).

CHAPTER 8

1. These disciples come in at least two varieties: the biological determinists so enamored with mental testing (who provide a "metal detector" that Plato would have found very useful), and the apologists for the traditional, elitist curriculum.

2. The "participatory paradigm" is an alternative to the "distributive paradigm" Young (1990a) uses to characterize traditional liberal views.

3. In this connection, my reading of the radical curriculum theorist Michael Apple (1993a, appendix) suggests that he concedes the leftist attack on liberal equality has proved a strategic mistake.

4. See Chapter 7 for a more detailed discussion.

References

Adelman, C. (1991). *Women at thirtysomething: Paradoxes of attainment*. Washington, DC: U.S. Department of Education.

Adler, M., & Associates. (1982). *The Paideia proposal: An educational manifesto*. New York: Macmillan.

Alston, K. (1995). The difference we make: Philosophy of education and the Tower of Babel. In W. Kohli (Ed.), *Critical conversations in philosophy of education* (pp. 278–299). New York: Routledge.

American Association of University Women (AAUW). (1991). *Shortchanging girls, shortchanging America*. Washington, DC: Author.

American Association of University Women (AAUW). (1993). *Hostile hallways*. Washington, DC: The American Association of University Women Educational Foundation.

Appiah, K. A. (1994). Identity, authenticity, survival: Multicultural societies and social reproduction. In A. Gutmann (Ed.), *Multiculturalism: Examining the politics of recognition* (pp. 149–163). Princeton, NJ: Princeton University Press.

Apple, M. (1988). *Teachers and texts: Political economy of class and gender relations*. New York: Routledge.

Apple, M. (1993a). *Official knowledge: Democratic education in a conservative age*. New York: Routledge.

Apple, M. (1993b). The politics of knowledge: Does a national curriculum make sense? *Teachers College Record, 95* (2), 222–241.

Aronowitz, S., & Giroux, H. (1991). *Postmodern education*. Minneapolis: University of Minnesota Press.

Bambrough, R. (Ed. and Trans.). (1963). *The philosophy of Aristotle*. New York: Signet.

Barber, B. (1992). *An aristocracy of everyone*. New York: Ballantine Books.

Baron, D. (1990). *The English-only question*. New Haven: Yale University Press.

Baynes, K., Bohman, J., & McCarthy, T. (1987). Michel Foucault. In K. Baynes, J. Bohman, & T. McCarthy (Eds.), *After philosophy: End or transformation?* (pp. 95–99). Cambridge, MA: MIT Press.

Beck, C. (1994). Postmodernism, pedagogy, and philosophy of education. In A. Thompson (Ed.), *Philosophy of Education 1993* (pp. 1–13). Urbana, IL: Philosophy of Education Society.

Belenky, M. F., Clinchy, B. McV., Goldberger, N. R., & Tarule, J. M. (1986). *Women's ways of knowing*. New York: Basic Books.

Benhabib, S. (1992). *Situating the self*. New York: Routledge.

Berliner, D., & Biddle, B. (1995). *The manufactured crisis*. Reading, MA: Addison-Wesley.

Bernstein, R. (1996, April). *Pragmatism and postmodernism: The relevance of John Dewey*. Paper presented at the meeting of the American Educational Research Association, New York.

Bierlein, L. A. (1996). *Charter schools: Initial findings*. Denver, CO: Education Commission of the States.

Bierlein, L. A., & Mulholland, L. A. (1994). The promise of charter schools. *Educational Leadership, 2*(1), 34–35, 37–40.

Bilingual Education Act, 20 U.S.C. § 3221 (1968).

Bowles, S., & Gintis, H. (1976). *Schooling in capitalist America*. New York: Basic Books.

Bowles, S., & Gintis, H. (1989). Can there be a liberal philosophy of education in a democratic society? In H. A. Giroux & P. McLaren (Eds.), *Critical pedagogy, the state, and cultural struggle* (pp. 24–31). Albany: State University of New York Press.

Bracey, G. (1992). The second Bracey report on the condition of public education. *Phi Delta Kappan ,74* (2), 104–117.

Bracey, G. (1994). The media's myth of school failure. *Educational Leadership, 52*(1), 80–84.

Brown v. Board of Education of Topeka, Kansas, 347 U.S. 483 (1954).

Brush, S. C. (1991). Women in science and engineering. *American Scientist, 79*, 404–419.

Bull, B. (1985). Eminence and precocity: An examination of the justification of education for the gifted and talented. *Teachers College Record, 87*(1), 1–19.

Burbules, N. (1990). Equal opportunity or equal education? *Educational Theory, 40*(2), 221–226.

Burbules, N. (1993).ı *Dialogue in teaching*. New York: Teachers College Press.

Burbules, N. (1996). Postmodern doubt and philosophy of education. In A. Neiman (Ed.), *Philosophy of education 1995* (pp. 39–48). Urbana, IL: Philosophy of Education Society.

Burbules, N., Lord, B., & Sherman, A. (1982). Equity, equal opportunity, and education. *Educational Evaluation and Policy Analysis, 4*(2), 169–187.

Burbules, N., & Rice, S. (1991). Dialogue across difference: Continuing the conversation. *Harvard Educational Review, 61*(4), 393–416.

Burbules, N., & Sherman, A. (1979). Equal educational opportunity: Ideal or ideology. In C. J. B. Macmillan (Ed.), *Philosophy of education 1979* (pp. 105–114). Urbana, IL: Philosophy of Education Society.

Camilli, G., & Shepard, L. (1994). *Methods for identifying biased test items*. Thousand Oaks, CA: Sage.

Chubb, J. E., & Moe, T. M. (1990). *Politics, markets and America's schools*. Washington, DC: Brookings Institution.

Coleman, J. (1968). The concept of equality of educational opportunity. *Harvard Educational Review, 38*(1), 7–22.

Coleman, J. (1990). Choice, community, and future schools. In W. H. Clune & J. G. Witte (Eds.), *Choice and control in American education* (vol. 1, pp. ix-xxii). New York: The Falmer Press.

Connell, R. W. (1987). *Gender and power*. Stanford, CA: Stanford University Press.

Connell, R. W. (1993). Disruptions: Improper masculinities and schooling. In L. Weis & M. Fine (Eds.), *Beyond Silenced Voices* (pp. 191-208). New York: State University of New York Press.

Cookson, P. W. (1992). The ideology of consumership and the coming deregulation of the public school system. In P. W. Cookson (Ed.), *The choice controversy* (pp. 83-102). Newbury Park, CA: Corwin Press.

Cookson, P. W. (1994). *School choice: The struggle for the soul of American education*. New Haven: Yale University Press.

Coons, J. E. (1990). As arrows in the hand. In W. H. Clune & J. G. Witte (Eds.), *Choice and control in American education* (vol. 1, pp. 319-326). New York: Falmer Press.

Coons, J. E., & Sugarman, S. D. (1978). *Education by choice: The case for family control*. Berkeley: University of California Press.

Cox, H. (1995). The warring versions of the religious right. *Atlantic Monthly, 276* (5), 59-69.

Curren, R. R. (1995). Justice and the threshold of educational equality. In M. S. Katz (Ed.), *Philosophy of education 1994* (pp. 239-248). Urbana, IL: Philosophy of Education Society.

Daniels, N. (1991). Meritocracy. In J. Arthur & W. H. Shaw (Eds.), *Justice and economic distribution* (2nd ed., pp. 154-167). Englewood Cliffs, NJ: Prentice-Hall.

Darling-Hammond, L. (1994). Performance based assessment and educational equity. *Harvard Educational Review, 64*(1), 5-30.

Delpit, L. (1993). The silenced dialogue: Power and pedagogy in educating other people's children. In L. Weis & M. Fine (Eds.), *Beyond silenced voices* (pp. 119-139). Albany: State University of New York Press.

Dennett, D. (1984). *Elbow room: The varieties of free will worth wanting* Cambridge, MA: MIT Press.

Dewey, J. (1922). *Human nature and conduct*. New York: Henry Holt.

Dewey, J. (1938). *Experience and education*. New York: Macmillan.

Dewey, J. (1946). *Problems of men*. New York: Philosophical Library.

Dewey, J. (1981a). Renascent liberalism. In J. J. McDermott (Ed.), *The philosophy of John Dewey* (pp. 647-648). Chicago: University of Chicago Press.

Dewey, J. (1981b). Search for the great community. In J. J. McDermott (Ed.), *The philosophy of John Dewey* (pp. 620-643). Chicago: University of Chicago Press.

Doll, W. (1993). *A post-modern perspective on curriculum*. New York: Teachers College Press.

Dworkin, R. M. (1977). *Taking rights seriously*. Cambridge, MA: Harvard University Press.

Eccles, J. (1989). Bringing young women into math and science. In M. Crawford & M. Gentry (Eds.), *Gender and thought* (pp. 36–58). New York: Springer-Verlag.

Education for All Handicapped Children Act, 20 U.S.C. § 1401 (1974).

Ellsworth, E. (1992). Why doesn't this feel empowering. In C. Luke & J. Gore (Eds.), *Feminisms and critical pedagogy* (pp. 90–119). New York: Routledge.

Elmore, R. (1994, March). *Opportunity to learn standards and education reform.* Paper presented at the meeting of the American Educational Research Association, New Orleans.

Elmore, R. F., & Fuller, B. (1996). Conclusion. In Fuller, B., Elmore R. F., & Orfield, G. (Eds.), *Who chooses? Who loses?* (pp. 187–201). New York: Teachers College Press.

Ennis, R. (1976). Equality of educational opportunity. *Educational Theory, 26*(1), 3–18.

Feingold, A. (1988). Cognitive gender differences are disappearing. *American Psychologist, 43*(2), 95–103.

Fetterman, D. M. (1988). *Excellence and equality: A qualitatively different perspective on gifted and talented education.* Albany: State University of New York Press.

Films for the Humanities, Inc. (1988). *Battle over the blackboard* [Videotape]. Princeton, NJ: Author.

Flanagan, O., & Jackson, K. (1990). Justice, care, and gender: The Kohlberg-Gilligan debate revisited. In C. R. Sunstein (Ed.), *Feminism and political theory* (pp. 37–52). Chicago: University of Chicago Press.

Fordham, S. (1993). Racelessness as a factor in black students' school success: Pragmatic strategy or Pyrrhic victory? In H. S. Shapiro & D. E. Purpel (Eds.), *Critical social issues in American education* (pp. 149–178). New York: Longman.

Foucault, M. (1987). Questions of method: An interview with Michel Foucault. In K. Baynes, J. Bohman, & T. McCarthy (Eds.), *After philosophy: End or transformation?* (pp. 100–117). Cambridge, MA: MIT Press.

Freire, P. (1983). Banking education. In H. Giroux & D. Purpel (Eds.), *The hidden curriculum and moral education* (pp. 283–291). Berkeley, CA: McCutchan.

Friend, R.A. (1993). Choices, not closets: Heterosexism and homophobia in schools. In L. Weis & M. Fine (Eds.), *Beyond silenced voices* (pp. 209–236). Albany: State University of New York Press.

Gallagher, J. J., & Gallagher, S. A. (1994). *Teaching the gifted* (4th ed.). Boston: Allyn and Bacon.

Garcia, G. E., & Pearson, P. D. (1994). Assessment and diversity. In L. Darling-Hammond (Ed.), *Review of research in education: Vol. 20* (pp. 337–393). Washington, D.C.: American Educational Research Association.

Gates, H. L., Jr. (1992). *Loose canons.* New York: Oxford University Press.

Gilligan, C. (1982). *In a different voice: Psychological theory and women's development.* Cambridge, MA: Harvard University Press.

Gilligan C. (1991). Teaching Shakespeare's sister: Notes from the underground of female adolescence. *Women's Studies Quarterly, 9*(1 & 2), 31–51.

Giroux, H. (1988). Border pedagogy in the age of postmodernism. *Journal of Education, 170*(3), 162–181.

Goodlad, J. I. (1984). *A place called school: Prospects for the future*. New York: McGraw-Hill.

Gould, S. J. (1981). *The mismeasure of man*. New York: W. W. Norton.

Green, T. (1983). Excellence, equity, and equality. In L. Shulman & G. Sykes (Eds.), *Handbook of teaching and educational policy* (pp. 318–341). New York: Longman.

Green, T. (1991). Excellence, equity, and equality clarified. In D. Ericson (Ed.), *Philosophy of education 1990* (pp. 220–224). Normal, IL: Philosophy of Education Society.

Gutmann, A. (1987). *Democratic education*. Princeton, NJ: Princeton University Press.

Gutmann, A. (1994). Introduction. In A. Gutmann (Ed.), *Multiculturalism: Examining the politics of recognition* (pp. 3–24). Princeton, NJ: Princeton University Press.

Habermas, J. (1994). Struggles for recognition in the democratic constitutional state. In A. Gutmann (Ed.), *Multiculturalism: Examining the politics of recognition* (pp. 107–148). Princeton, NJ: Princeton University Press.

Hallinan, M. T. (1994a). School differences in tracking effects of achievement. *Social Forces, 72* (3), 799–820.

Hallinan, M. T. (1994b). Tracking: From theory to practice. *Sociology of Education, 67*(2), 79–84.

Hampshire, S. (1983). *Morality and conflict*. Cambridge, MA: Harvard University Press.

Haney, W. (1984). Testing reasoning and reasoning about testing. *Review of Educational Research, 54*(4), 597–654.

Haney, W. (1993). Testing and minorities. In L. Weis & M. Fine (Eds.), *Beyond silenced voices* (pp. 45–74) . Albany: State University of New York Press.

Hedges, L. V., Laine, R. D., & Greenwald, R. (1994). Does money matter? A meta-analysis of studies of the effects of differential school inputs on student outcomes. *Educational Researcher, 23*(3), 5–14.

Henig, J. (1994). *Rethinking school choice*. Princeton, NJ: Princeton University Press.

Hirsch, E. D. (1988). *Cultural literacy*. New York: Vintage Books.

Hirsch, E. D. (Ed.). (1993). *What your first grader needs to know.* New York: Dell.

Holland, D., & Eisenhart, M. (1990). *Educated in romance*. Chicago: University of Chicago Press.

House, E. (1991). Big policy, little policy. *Educational Researcher, 20*(5), 21–26.

House, E., & Howe, K. R. (1990). Second chance in educational policy. In D. Inbar (Ed.), *Second chance in education* (pp. 49–65). New York: The Falmer Press.

Houston, B. (1988). Gilligan and the politics of a distinctive women's morality. In L. Code, S. Mullett, & C. Overall (Eds.), *Feminist perspectives: Philosophical essays on method and morals* (pp. 168–189). Toronto: University of Toronto Press.

Howe, K. R. (1985). Two dogmas of educational research. *Educational Researcher,* *14*(8), 10–18.

Howe, K. R. (1989). In defense of outcomes-based conceptions of equal educational opportunity. *Educational Theory, 39*(4), 317–336.

Howe, K. R. (1990). Equal opportunity *is* equal education (within limits). *Educational Theory, 40*(2), 227–230.

Howe, K. R. (1992). Getting over the quantitative-qualitative debate. *American Journal of Education, 100*(2), 236–256.

Howe, K. R., & Eisenhart, M. (1990). Standards for qualitative (and quantitative) research: A prolegomenon. *Educational Researcher, 9*(4), 2–9.

Howe, K. R., & Miramontes, O. B. (1992). *The ethics of special education.* New York: Teachers College Press.

Jaggar, A. (1983). *Feminist politics and human nature.* Totowa, NJ: Rowan and Littlefield.

Jencks, C. (1988). Whom must we treat equally for educational opportunity to be equal? *Ethics, 98*(3), 518–533.

Kane, J. (1992). Choice: The fundamentals revisited. In P. W. Cookson (Ed.), *The choice controversy* (pp. 46–63). Newbury Park, CA: The Corwin Press.

Keyes v. School District No. 1, 413 U.S. 189 (1973).

Kirp, D. L. (1992). What school choice really means. *Atlantic, 270*(5), 119–132.

Klein, S. S., & Ortman, P. (1994). Continuing the journey toward gender equity. *Educational Researcher, 2*(8), 13–21.

Kozol, J. (1991). *Savage inequalities.* New York: Crown.

Kozol J. (1993). Savage inequalities: An interview with Jonathan Kozol. *Educational Theory, 43*(1), 55–70.

Kunc, N. (1992, March). *The importance of belonging.* Lecture presented to St. Vrain School District, Longmont, CO.

Kymlicka, W. (1990). *Contemporary political theory: An introduction.* New York: Oxford University Press.

Kymlicka, W. (1991). *Liberalism, community, and culture.* New York: Oxford University Press.

Kymlicka, W. (1995). *Multicultural citizenship: A liberal theory of minority rights.* New York: Oxford University Press.

Larmore, C. (1987). *Patterns of moral complexity.* New York: Cambridge University Press.

Lather, P. (1991a). *Getting smart: Feminist research and pedagogy with/in postmodernism.* New York: Routledge.

Lather, P. (1991b). Post-critical pedagogies: A feminist reading. *Education and Society, 9* (2), 100–111.

Lau v. Nichols, 414 U.S. 563 (1974).

Leo, J. (1993, June 14). Democrats weaken school reform plan. *Daily Camera,* p. 3c.

Levin, H. (1990). The theory of choice applied to education. In W. H. Clune & J. G. Witte (Eds.), *Choice and control in American education* (vol. 1, pp. 247–284). New York: Falmer Press.

Levin, M. (1981). Equality of opportunity. *Philosophical Quarterly, 31*(123), 110–125.

Lindsay, D. (1995). Wisconsin, Ohio back vouchers for religious schools. *Education Week, 14*(40), 1, 14.

Linn, M. C., & Hyde, J. S. (1989). Gender, mathematics, and science. *Educational Researcher 18*(8), 17–19, 22–27.

Linn, M. C., & Petersen, A. C. (1985). Facts and assumptions about the nature of sex differences. In S. S. Klein (Ed.), *Handbook for achieving sex equity through education* (pp. 53–77). Baltimore: Johns Hopkins University Press.

Lyon, D. (1994). *Postmodernity*. Minneapolis: University of Minnesota Press.

Lyotard, J. (1987). The postmodern condition. In K. Baynes, J. Bohman, & T. McCarthy (Eds.), *After philosophy: End or transformation?* (pp. 67–94). Cambridge, MA: MIT Press.

MacIntyre, A. (1981). *After virtue*. Notre Dame, IN: University of Notre Dame Press.

MacIntyre, A. (1987). The idea of an educated public. In G. Haydon (Ed.), *Education and values* (pp. 15–36). London: Institute of Education, University of London.

MacNeil, R. (Executive Producer). (1995, January 12). *The MacNeil/Lehrer news hour*. New York and Washington, DC: Public Broadcasting Service.

Madaus, G. (1994). A technological and historical consideration of equity issues associated with proposals to change the nation's testing policy. *Harvard Educational Review, 64*(1), 76–95.

Maker, C. J., & Schiever, S. W. (Eds.). (1989). *Critical issues in special education: Defensible programs for cultural and ethnic minorities*. Austin, TX: PRO-ED.

Martin, J. R. (1982). The educated person. In D. DeNicola (Ed.), *Philosophy of Education 1981* (pp. 3–20). Normal, IL: Philosophy of Education Society.

Martin, J. R. (1992). *The schoolhome: Rethinking schools for changing families*. Cambridge, MA: Harvard University Press.

Martin, J. R. (1994). *Changing the educational landscape*. New York: Routledge.

McCarthy, C. (1993). Beyond the poverty in race relations: Nonsynchrony and social difference in education. In L. Weis & M. Fine (Eds.), *Beyond Silenced Voices* (pp. 325–346). Albany: State University of New York Press.

McLaren, P. (1988). Schooling the postmodern body: Critical pedagogy and the politics of enfleshment. *Journal of Education, 170*(3), 53–83.

Messick, S. (1989). Validity. In R. L. Linn (Ed.), *Educational measurement* (3rd ed., pp. 13–103). New York: American Council on Education and Macmillan.

Mill, J. S. (1992). The subjection of women. In J. P. Sterba (Ed.), *Justice: Alternative perspectives* (pp. 275–284). Belmont, CA: Wadsworth. (Original work published 1869)

Murray, C., & Herrnstein, R. (1994). *The bell curve*. New York: The Free Press.

Nagel, T. (1986). *The view from nowhere*. New York: Oxford University Press.

Nagel, T. (1991). *Justice and partiality*. New York: Oxford University Press.

National Commission on Excellence in Education (1983). *A nation at risk*. Washington, DC: U. S. Government Printing Office.

National Council of Education Standards and Testing (NCEST). (1992). *Raising standards for American education*. Washington, DC: Author.

Noddings, N. (1984). *Caring: A feminist approach to ethics and moral education*. Berkeley: University of California Press.

Noddings, N. (1990). Feminist critiques in the professions. In C. Cadzen (Ed.), *Review of research in education: Vol. 16* (pp. 393–424). Washington, DC: American Educational Research Association.

Noddings, N. (1992). *The challenge to care in schools*. New York: Teachers College Press.

Noddings, N. (1993a). *Educating for intelligent belief or disbelief*. New York: Teachers College Press.

Noddings, N. (1993b). Excellence as a guide to educational conversation. In H. A. Alexander (Ed.), *Philosophy of education 1992* (pp. 5–16). Urbana, IL: Philosophy of Education Society.

Nozick, R. (1974). *Anarchy, state, and utopia*. New York: Basic Books.

Oakes, J. (1985). *Keeping track: How schools structure inequality*. New Haven, CT: Yale University Press.

Oakes, J. (1987). Tracking in secondary schools: A contextual perspective. *Educational Psychologist, 22*(2), 129–153.

Oakes, J. (1990). Opportunities, achievement, and choice: Women and minorities in science and mathematics. In C. Cadzen (Ed.), *Review of research in education: Vol. 16* (pp. 153–222). Washington, DC: American Educational Research Association.

Oakes, J. (1994). More than misapplied technology: A normative and political response to Hallinan on tracking. *Sociology of Education, 67*(2), 84–89.

Oakes, J., Ormseth, T., Bell, R., & Camp, P. (1990). *Multiplying inequalities: The effects of race, social class, and tracking on opportunities to learn mathematics and science*. Washington, DC: The Rand Corporation.

Ogbu, J. (1992). Understanding cultural diversity and learning. *Educational Researcher, 21*(8), 5–14.

Ogbu, J., & Matute-Bianchi, M. (1986). Understanding sociocultural factors: Knowledge, identity, and school adjustment. In *Beyond language: Social and cultural factors in schooling language minority students* (pp. 73–142). Los Angeles: California State University, Evaluation, Dissemination and Assessment Center.

Okin, S. M. (1989). *Justice, gender, and the family*. New York: Basic Books.

O'Neill, O. (1976). Opportunities, equalities, and education. *Theory and Decision, 7*(4), 275–295.

Page, R. (1976). Opportunity and its willing requirement. In K. Strike (Ed.), *Philosophy of Education 1976* (pp. 296–309). Urbana, IL: Philosophy of Education Society.

Pearson, J. (1993). *Myths of educational choice*. Westport, CT: Praeger.

Pitsch, M. (1995a). Bill to push block grant for education. *Education Week, 14*(41), 1, 31.

Pitsch, M. (1995b). Goals 2000 column stirs the political pot. *Education Week, 15*(10), 19.

Plessy v. Ferguson, 163 U.S. 537 (1896).

Ravitch, D. (1990, Summer). Multiculturalism: E pluribus plures. *American Scholar*, 337–356.

Ravitch, D. (1994). Somebody's children. *Network News and Views, 13*(11), 112–118.

Rawls, J. (1971). *A theory of justice*. Cambridge, MA: The Belknap Press.

Rawls, J. (1985). Justice as fairness: Political, not metaphysical. *Philosophy and Public Affairs, 14*(3), 223–251.

Rawls, J. (1993). *Political liberalism*. New York: Columbia University Press.

Raywid, M. A. (1990). Is there a case for choice? *Educational Leadership, 48*(4), 4–12.

Raywid, M. A. (1994). Alternative schools: The state of the art. *Educational Leadership, 52*(1), 26–31.

Resnick, L. B., & Resnick, D. P. (1992). Assessing the thinking curriculum: New tools for educational reform. In B. R. Gifford & M. C. O'Connor (Eds.), *Changing assessments: Alternative views of aptitude, achievement and instruction* (pp. 37–75). Boston: Kluwer Academic.

Richards, J. R. (1980). *The skeptical feminist: A philosophical inquiry*. London: Routledge and Kegan Paul.

Richert, E. S. (1991). Rampant problems and promising practices in identification. In N. A. Colangelo & G. A. Davis (Eds.), *Handbook of gifted education* (pp. 81–96). Boston: Allyn and Bacon.

Riordan, C. (1990). *Girls and boys in school: Together or separate?* New York: Teachers College Press.

Rodriguez, R. (1982). *Hunger of memory: The education of Richard Rodriguez*. Boston: David R. Godine.

Rothman, R. (1994). Assessment questions: Equity answers. In *Evaluation comment: Proceedings of the 1993 CRESST Conference* (pp. 1–12). Los Angeles: UCLA, Center for the Study of Evaluation & The National Center for Research on Evaluation, Standards, and Student Testing.

Sadker, M., & Sadker, D. (1986). Sexism in the classroom: From grade school to graduate school. *Phi Delta Kappan, 67*, 512–516.

Sadker, M., & Sadker, D. (1994). *Failing at fairness: How America's schools cheat girls*. New York: Scribner's.

Salamone, R. (1986). *Equal education under the law*. New York: St. Martin's Press.

Sandel, M. (1982). *Liberalism and the limits of justice*. Cambridge: Cambridge University Press.

Sapon-Shevin, M. (1994). *Playing favorites: Gifted education and the disruption of community*. Albany: State University of New York Press.

Schlesinger, A. M., Jr. (1992). *The disuniting of America: Reflections on a multicultural society*. New York: W. W. Norton.

Schrag, F. (1992). In defense of positivist research paradigms. *Educational Researcher, 21* (5), 5–8.

Shakeshaft, C. (1986). A gender at risk. *Phi Delta Kappan, 67*, 499–503.

Shepard, L. (1993). Evaluating test validity. In L. Darling-Hammond (Ed.), *Review of research in education: Vol. 19* (pp. 405–450). Washington, DC: American Educational Research Association.

Shofield, J. W. (1991). School desegregation and intergroup relations. In G. Grant (Ed.), *Review of research in education: Vol. 17* (pp. 335–412). Washington, DC: American Educational Research Association.

Spring, J. (1984). Education and the Sony war. *Phi Delta Kappan, 65*(8), 534–537.

Spring, J. (1989). *The sorting machine revisited* (Rev. ed.). New York: Longman.

Strike, K. (1984). Is there a conflict between equity and excellence? *Educational Evaluation and Policy Analysis, 7*(4), 409–415.

Strike, K. A. (1988). The ethics of resource allocation in education. In D. H. Monk & J. Underwood (Eds.), *Microlevel school finance: Issues and implications for policy* (pp. 143–180). Cambridge, MA: Ballinger.

Strike, K. A. (1991). The moral role of schooling in a liberal democratic society. In G. Grant (Ed.), *Review of research in education: Vol. 17* (pp. 413–483). Washington, DC: American Educational Research Association.

Stromquist, N. P. (1993). Sex-equity legislation in education: The state as promoter of women's rights. *Review of Educational Research, 63*(4), 379–407.

Tannenbaum, A. J. (1991). The social psychology of giftedness. In N. Colangelo & G. A. Davis (Eds.), *Handbook of gifted education* (pp. 27–44). Boston: Allyn and Bacon.

Taylor, C. (1989). Cross-purposes: The liberal-communitarian debate. In N. L. Rosenblum (Ed.), *Liberalism and the moral life* (pp. 159–182). Cambridge, MA: Harvard University Press.

Taylor, C. (1994). The politics of recognition. In A. Gutmann (Ed.), *Multiculturalism: Examining the politics of recognition* (pp. 25–74). Princeton, NJ: Princeton University Press.

Taylor, C. (1995). *Philosophical arguments*. Cambridge, MA: Harvard University Press.

Tierney, W. G. (1993). The college experience of Native Americans: A critical analysis. In L. Weis & M. Fine (Eds.), *Beyond silenced voices* (pp. 309–324). Albany: State University of New York Press.

Title IX of the Education Amendments, 20 U.S.C. § 1681 (1972).

Treffinger, D. J. (1991). Future goals and directions. In N. Colangelo & G. A. Davis (Eds.), *Handbook of gifted education* (pp. 441–449). Boston: Allyn and Bacon.

U.S. Department of Education (1991). *America 2000*. Washington, DC: U.S. Government Printing Office.

U.S. Department of Education and Office of Bilingual Education and Minority Language Affairs (1995). *Digest of educational statistics for limited English proficient students*. Washington, DC: National Clearing House for Bilingual Education.

U.S. House of Representatives (1994a). *Goals 2000: Educate America Act*, Conference Report Notes, Part B, Report 103–446. Washington, DC: Author.

U.S. House of Representatives (1994b). *Goals 2000: Educate America fact sheet*. (ERIC Document Reproduction Service).

Usher, R., & Edwards, R. (1994). *Postmodernism and education*. New York: Routledge.

Walzer, M. (1983). *Spheres of justice: A defense of pluralism and equality*. New York: Basic Books.

Walzer, M. (1987). *Interpretation and social criticism*. Cambridge, MA: Harvard University Press.

Weiler, K. (1988). *Women teaching for change*. South Hadley, MA: Bergin and Garvey.

Wells, A. S. (1993). *Time to choose*. New York: Hill and Wang.

Wells, A. S., & Crain, R.L. (1992). Do parents choose school quality or school status: A sociological theory of free market education. In P. W. Cookson (Ed.), *The choice controversy* (pp. 65–82). Newbury Park, CA: The Corwin Press.

West, C. (1992). Black leadership and the pitfalls of racial reasoning. In T. Morrison (Ed.), *Race-ing justice, en-gendering power* (pp. 390–401). New York: Pantheon Books.

Willis, S. (1995). Charter schools take hold. *Education Update, 37*(8): 1, 4–5, 8.

Wisconsin v. Yoder, 406 U.S. 205 (1972).

Witte, J. (1990). Choice and control: An analytic overview. In W. Clune & J. Witte (Eds.), *Choice and control in American education* (vol. 1, pp. 11–46). New York: Falmer Press.

Wolf, S. (1994). Comment. In A. Gutmann (Ed.), *Multiculturalism: An examination of the politics of recognition* (pp. 75–86). Princeton, N. J.: Princeton University Press.

Young, I. M. (1990a). *Justice and the politics of difference*. Princeton, NJ: Princeton University Press.

Young, I. M. (1990b). *Throwing like a girl and other essays in philosophy and social theory*. Bloomington: Indiana University Press.

Young, R. (1990). *A critical theory of education*. New York: Teachers College Press.

Index

About the Author

Kenneth R. Howe is an associate professor at the School of Education, University of Colorado–Boulder. Since taking his doctorate in philosophy and education from Michigan State University in 1985, he has co-authored (with Ofelia Miramontes) *The Ethics of Special Education* and published more than forty papers on equal educational opportunity and other philosophical topics in refereed journals and contributed volumes. His research areas include the philosophy of educational research, applied and professional ethics, and the philosophy of education.